"This is one of the most practic
available for anyone who want

New York Times bestselling author of
Crucial Conversations and *Change Anything*

"Often it's the simple daily doses of small loving actions that nurture a relationship. [This] is a celebration of the little things that can make love last. Filled with the latest marriage research, personal stories, and anecdotes from happy partners, this book contains everyday tools that can actually make a difference."

—**Margaret Paul, PhD**,
best-selling author of *Do I Have to Give
Up Me To Be Loved By You?*, *Healing Your Aloneness*,
and *Inner Bonding*

"Most self-help books are written by clinicians. Few topics in the relationship arena are examined by those in the 'trenches of life.' Heidi Poelman is a rather typical middle-class American wife and mother. She writes as one experiencing marriage as it is—with highs and lows—yet her approach is about what works. Her positive style offers suggestion after suggestion to the reader about how to give and receive love in ways that offer hope and direction to all those wanting to be happily married. This is a wonderful book, full of little gems and nuggets of wisdom. I endorse it for those young and old who want to stay content in a committed relationship."

—**J. Kent Griffiths, PhD**,
Marriage and family therapist

The TWO MiNUTE SECRET to Staying iN Love

Copyright © 2016 by Heidi Poelman

All rights reserved.

Published by Familius LLC, www.familius.com

Familius books are available at special discounts for bulk purchases, whether for sales promotions or for family or corporate use. For more information, contact Familius Sales at 559-876-2170 or e-mail orders@familius.com.

Library of Congress Cataloging-in-Publication Data

LCCN: 2016962612

Print ISBN 9781945547058

Ebook ISBN 9781945547409

Hardcover ISBN 9781945547416

Printed in the United States of America

Edited by Katie Arnold

Cover design by David Miles

Book design by Kurt Wahlner

10 9 8 7 6 5 4 3 2

Second Edition

The TWO MINUTE SECRET to Staying in Love

SIMPLE, POWERFUL WAYS TO MAKE YOUR MARRIAGE LAST

Heidi Poelman

This book is dedicated to Scott,
my husband and best friend,
who has taught me so much about how to love
and the joy of being loved in return.

Contents

Preface

I recently sat down to tackle my weekly—and despised—job of paying for life's bills. We've all been there: paying the credit card balances, checking receipts, moving money around, mailing checks, balancing the books—it's the responsible stuff of life. I've never liked this job, but alas, I figured the alternative of not doing it would probably be worse, at least eventually. I took a deep breath, turned on my laptop, and opened the finances folder on my desk. Inside the folder, I found a small, white piece of paper. Written in blue pen was this: *Dearest Heidi, I love you so much. You are my dream girl.* That tiny note flipped the whole moment upside down. Suddenly, I was smiling.

Those words might sound like the sort of thing that comes in the early stages of romance, when star-crossed lovers have fallen head over heels, think of nothing else, and write mushy messages to one another. In this case, the mushy message was from my husband of sixteen years—the man who swept me off my feet, married me, finished graduate school next to me, bought a home with me, entered parenthood with me, and continues to teach me about the kind of person I want to be.

The secret to having an amazing, intimate, playful, and happy marriage is not as complicated as you may think. In fact, as it turns out, experts and people in loving marriages seem to agree: the secret to staying in love comes down to the little things, even something as small as a love note in a finances folder. That same piece of paper has impacted me over and over, every time I sit down to pay the bills. How long did it take for my husband to write those two sentences? I don't know—how long did it take you to read them? Less than two minutes, I'd wager. Yet the ripples of that tiny drop of thoughtfulness have a much larger impact.

As you may have noticed, our day and age is anything but simple. We live in a chaotic and distracting world with seemingly endless pressures and responsibilities. Hundreds of things are competing for our attention, and we are connected to more people, places, and ideas than ever before. Yet, in marriage, many partners find themselves drifting apart. A huge number are either calling it quits or living unhappy and unfulfilled. No one plans that. Most of us marry with hopes of a lasting and fulfilling partnership. Falling in love was easy. Why is staying in love so hard? Where did the promise of a happy, intimate, playful, and passionate relationship go?

Before we married, my husband, Scott, and I read several marriage books to help us prepare. But after getting thrown into the thralls of real life, jobs, bills, and kids, I found that the details from those books were a little fuzzy. I vaguely remembered theories on conflict management, dialogue patterns, and constant selflessness. Those are all fine and good, but I wanted something simpler. After all, love is simple, isn't it? I wanted something that I could use regularly to refresh my couple-connection skills—something that spelled out the small but meaningful things I could do every day to strengthen my marriage. I wanted the simple secrets. What is it that happy couples do to stand the test of time?

My interest started in graduate school where, whenever I had the chance, I pored over studies on marriage communication. I found it fascinating that something as simple as asking for an opinion could have a dramatic effect on feelings of fairness in a relationship. Only recently, after several more years of marriage and four kids in tow, did I decide to whittle down my findings and experiences in a book that could actually help couples. I got to work reviewing the latest books from the experts, reading more marriage studies, and interviewing happy couples to find the everyday tools that work in the real world. I pondered my own experiences to distill exactly what it is that makes me feel loved—and *in* love. My conclusion was refreshing and relevant for every couple who wants to stay in love for the long haul. It comes down to this: the little things we think, say, and do in marriage create the heartbeat that keeps love alive.

We all want the big things: happiness, intimacy, loyalty, friendship, excitement, and passion. The small and simple things in marriage are the stepping stones that pave the way to a fantastic partnership. It's the way he tells her she's beautiful when she comes down the stairs and the way she hugs him at the door when he comes home. It's the way he brings home her favorite pint of ice cream as a surprise and the way she calls to ask how his day is going. It's the way she asks whether he would prefer blue walls or green and the way he checks in to let her know he'll be home late. It's the way she laughs at his jokes—even the not-so-funny ones—and the way he looks at her and thinks to himself *I am the luckiest man alive*, even when he knows all her flaws. By creating a marriage filled with little gestures of affection, respect, gratitude, and friendship, we are laying the path to lasting, amazing love and all the big things that go along with it.

This is how the marriage experts sum things up: Dr. John Gottman, who has studied couples for forty years in his "love lab," writes, "Here's the truth about marriage. It's the *small, positive things*, done often, that make all the difference." Dr. John Jacobs, a marriage therapist and psychiatry professor at NYU Medical College, advises his clients who want to stay in love to simply go home with a little gift, express a heartfelt thanks, or give a sincere compliment. He explains, "The simple truth is that *it doesn't take that much* to give your spouse the sense that he or she is very important to you." Marriage researchers Carol Bruess and Anna Kudak write, "Find pleasure in even the *smallest* gestures, jobs, and routines of your marriage. There you will find your *greatest* joys." *New York Times* reporter Tara Parker-Pope reviewed hundreds of studies on marriage and came to this conclusion: "What marital science teaches us is that improving a marriage doesn't require sweeping changes. Couples in good marriages get *the little things* right."

With this book, I hope to tell a staying-in-love story that is relevant and easy to use for every couple, from newlyweds to those who have been married for decades. These are the simple tools for building a loving and lasting connection. Though they are bite-sized, these marriage tips are actually quite filling; they are easy to learn, easy to remember, easy to do, and full of impact.

The title of this book does not suggest that having a fantastic, strong, and loving marriage is easy or that quick, mindless acts can change a relationship. This book is not advice for just how little affection you can get away with. Marriage is the single most important relationship in our lives, and that relationship deserves all the time, effort, and attention we can give. I believe in regular date nights, annual getaways, and spending as much time together as life allows. The two-minute focus is for this simple reason: in the chaos and distraction of our busy lives, the little things really do make a difference. They always have.

A note to those of you who think the problems in your marriage are too big for any simple act to make a difference—this project is not about a simple act. It is about intentionally doing the little things that affect the environment of your marriage over time. When I first shared the idea of writing about the little things in marriage with a skeptical friend who has struggled to keep a loving marriage, his initial response was, "Well, that's great for healthy people in healthy relationships, but it's too simple for couples with real issues." After I started asking him how he felt loved, he became filled with emotion expressing how much it means to him when his wife sits down, looks him in the eye, and asks, "So how was your day?" Yes, some couples have big obstacles in the road. But with a commitment to loving, forgiving, and forging a new path, the little things might just change everything.

The two-minute secret to staying passionately in love comes down to this: learn how to deliberately love and cherish your spouse in small, meaningful ways every day. These moments are probably the things that helped you fall in love in the first place. Whether it's a hug at the door, a love note on the mirror, an expression of gratitude, a sincere apology, or a simple call to say "hello," these are the things that keep love alive. Like fuel on a fire, these connections can keep love burning strong. Read on, experiment, and see what happens—your marriage is worth it.

Chapter 1

First Comes Love, Then Comes Marriage... Then What?

Oh, now you are mine! At last you are mine!
Soon—in a few months, perhaps, my angel
will sleep in my arms, will awaken in my arms,
will live there. All your thoughts at all moments,
all your looks will be for me; all my thoughts, all
my moments, all my looks will be for you!

—**Victor Hugo**, FRENCH WRITER AND POET

Do you remember falling in love? Do you remember how you felt when you realized you had finally found The One? You probably saw life in rose-colored perfection and knew that your story, against all odds, would end in "happily ever after." The night my husband, Scott, and I met at a college barbecue, no one could break us apart. We were entranced. It wasn't long before we were completely enamored and could hardly think of anything besides being together. Romantic strolls, lengthy phone calls, and heart-melting poetry paved the way toward our wedding day. Sure, there were a few bumps in the road (actually, one big bump, as we both had to resolve the fear stemming from two sets of divorced parents). But when we ultimately vowed to love each other forever, we literally could not have been happier. It seems that's how most love stories go.

What happens next in the story? What happened to Cinderella and her prince after the honeymoon was over? Did he go off to fight important battles and lose himself in ruling a kingdom? Did she get swept up in visiting the nobles and planning the next royal ball? Does the magic stick around?

Not long after Scott and I sealed the deal, we slowly came to realize just how imperfect we both are and that we didn't always agree on everything. There were even times when (gasp) we wanted to be alone. Our love story began to include a little less heart-throbbing magic and a little more scheduling, disagreeing, compromising, dishwashing, cleaning, bill paying, and all the normal stuff of real life. Staying in love is harder than falling in love, no doubt about it. But here's the great thing: with all the shared experiences, memories, and connection that comes from joining two lives into one, our love story also grew to include more depth and more joy.

Building a happy courtship that stands the test of time is possible. It simply requires ongoing effort and some understanding of that crazy, amazing, head-spinning, transformative thing we call "love."

"Falling" in Love

As unromantic as it sounds, falling in love is partly a biological function of the brain. We are wired to fall hard for Miss or Mister Right. Researchers who have studied the brain chemistry of people falling in love have found that our brains actually start behaving like people with Obsessive-Compulsive Disorder. We become irrational, we can't stop thinking about each other, we call repeatedly, we want to be together incessantly, and we are over-the-top delighted to see each other, even if we've only been apart for an hour. As George Bernard Shaw humorously pointed out, marriage brings together two people "under the influence of the most violent, most insane, most delusive, and most transient of passions. They are required to swear that they will remain in that excited, abnormal, and exhausting condition continuously until death do them part."

I've been there. When we were falling hard, Scott and I had to be together every available minute of the day. When he went on a study-abroad trip to London (which he of course had planned before we met), he sent me a postcard every single day. We sent e-mails or chatted by instant message every single night. Our biology was pushing us together, subconsciously motivating us to connect.

Let's be clear: I believe that falling in love is far more significant and special than a brain function alone. It is a wonderful part of being human, with all the intertwining emotions and dreams that go along with it. After all, people don't fall in love every day. In some ways, it seems like a small miracle when one person falls in love with another who loves them back. I had never in my life met someone who knocked me off my feet like Scott did. Falling in love with "The One" is something to celebrate.

The reality is, though, we aren't quite ourselves when we are swept away. We become lost in new feelings of excitement and affection. The highs of falling in love don't last. Researchers who study the effects of love have found that the affectionate honeymoon stage of marriage lasts only about two years. After two years of wedded bliss, people typically revert back to however happy or unhappy they were before they fell in love. Then, often, they get lazy about love. Their brains just aren't pushing them anymore.

As marriage therapists Harville Hendrix and Helen LaKelly Hunt say in their book *Making Marriage Simple*, "Romantic love sticks around long enough to bind two people together. Then it rides off into the sunset." Unfortunately for so many, marriage doesn't prove to be the "happily ever after" they signed up for.

Falling in love is easy. Our body, brain, and heart are swimming with affection. Those feelings, early on, make it easy to show our love in regular doses every day. Partners effortlessly connect with heartfelt embraces, phone calls, compliments, surprises, and love letters. In marriage, those loving feelings may ebb and flow, but partners make a promise to love each other through good and bad. My friend Sarah told me how important that commitment has been in her twenty-year marriage. She said, "On the day Clint and I got married, he pulled me aside and said, 'No matter what you do, I will never leave you.' I wish I had understood at that moment what an amazing gift he was giving me." Marriage is not a certificate for guaranteed falling-in-love feelings till death do us part. Marriage is a commitment to keep on loving.

What's Love Got to Do with It?

Right now in the United States there are more than sixty million married couples. Clearly, as a country, we still love and believe in marriage. We love marriage so much that we fight over how to define it and exactly who can do it. However, by most accounts, marriage today is not thriving. Experts calculate that only about 40 to 50 percent of married couples will stay together.[5] People quit their marriages every day, and here's the sad thing: the majority of people who quit simply fell out of love. More than half the couples who get divorced had a relationship that was "amiable but listless." Basically, they just didn't thrive. They didn't feel the love.

According to studies on these couples, the vast majority of people who end their relationship report that they simply lost a sense of closeness and did not feel loved or appreciated. Even many couples that stay together aren't fulfilled in their marriages. Of the couples that do stay married, research suggests that only half are actually happy.

What is going on? Most people, at least in the western world, marry because they are in love and want to build a happy life together. That wasn't always the case. For thousands of years, marriage wasn't about love or personal satisfaction. According to historian Stephanie Coontz, marrying for love didn't come about until the late eighteenth century with the Enlightenment's focus on individual rights and the pursuit of happiness. Before then, most marriages were arranged by outside influences that would be positively affected by the union. Something as important as marriage couldn't be based on "something as unreasoning and transitory as love." During the Enlightenment, a marriage revolution began to occur. We started seeing marriage as what it could be—a private relationship with the potential to provide great joy for the couple, regardless of family wealth or political alliances.

Staying in Love

So the idea of a love-based marriage took root. We decided that it should be in our control as individuals to choose whom we marry and that we should do it primarily for our own happiness and not for the betterment of our relatives or communities. We decided that marriage could be our greatest human relationship and the source of our deepest satisfaction in life. Yet, as Coontz reports, "the very features that promised to make marriage such a unique and treasured personal relationship opened the way for it to become an optional and fragile one." Marriages are breaking apart today because people are falling out of love, and love is supposed to be the sticking force.

We "fall" in love, suggesting that it is something outside of our control. Our brain is malfunctioning, to a degree. Eventually, we become ourselves again, and we are left with an amazing possibility—the possibility of lasting love. It's a different kind of love, yes. Mature love is less the fiery flames of passion and more the hot coals of deep, committed connection. Dr. John Gottman, one of the world's leading marriage experts, who has studied married couples for more than forty years, says the basis of successful marriages can be summed up in a word: friendship. Happily married couples respect each other, like being with each other, and want each other's happiness.

Whether a couple's romantic love evolves into a deep, affectionate friendship isn't about luck, and it doesn't happen on its own. Staying together in our modern day takes more meaningful effort than it used to. Over the years, as a culture, we have lost some of the glue that used to help couples stick together. At least in western culture, we no longer live in a time when our parents, our society, our customs, our government, or our religions weld two people together. We are on our own to make it work. As John Jacobs writes, the only glue holding couples together now "is the glue created by the two of you—the glue of mutual satisfaction, gratification, appreciation, and respect. The glue of mature love."

The "glue" that keeps us together goes in what therapists Harville Hendrix and Helen LaKelly Hunt call the "Space in Between." They actually describe the physics of the space between two partners as a field with a force and energy. Consider what you see when you look out into the night sky with all the planets and stars and galaxies. We used to think the space between two objects was just emptiness. Now we know that there is a force between everything, either pushing it together or pulling it apart. This space between husband and wife is where we can make an impact. We create either loving fondness or frustrated disdain. Either we push ourselves apart with tension and negativity or we pull ourselves closer in an environment of connectedness and affection. Every little thing we do affects this space, for better or worse. As Hendrix and Hunt put it, "Every word, tone of voice, every glance, affects the Space Between." The little things have great power to connect us or, in their absence, let us drift apart. We must constantly be asking ourselves, *What am I doing to affect the space between my spouse and me?*

What's in It for Me?

Ask yourself again: do you remember falling in love? Do you remember how wonderful it felt? Do you remember your shared dreams and your hopes for the future? Do you remember why you wanted to join your lives? We are the captains of our fate, the makers of our own marital glue. We get to decide if we are willing to put in the effort required for real, lasting love. Staying in love isn't as easy or effortless as falling in love, and sticking together isn't as easy as it used to be. Building a love that lasts takes time, attention, and deliberate effort, but it doesn't take long. The effort to stay in love can be made in small, meaningful thoughts, words, and actions every day. If we do it right, our relationship can provide the same joyful excitement as it did when we first came together as partners, soul mates, and best friends. Indeed, if we do it right, and if we do it consistently, staying in love with our spouse can be the happiest, most fulfilling part of our lives. The trick is to do that even while living in a chaotic, modern world that is constantly pulling our attention elsewhere.

TWO-MINUTE ACTION STEPS

(COMPLETE ONCE AND REPEAT OFTEN):

Look back on how you met your spouse and what it felt like to fall in love. Make a commitment to do what is required to stay in love.

Consider what feelings you want in the space between you and your spouse. Do you want to feel loved? Respected? Cherished? How do you want your spouse to feel? Write down your thoughts.

Where do you want your marriage to be in five years? Ten years? Write down your goals for your relationship's future.

Chapter 2

Have You Got a Minute? Why Little Things Matter So Much

It's the little details that are vital. Little things make big things happen.

—John Wooden,

UCLA BASKETBALL COACH AND WINNER

OF 10 NCAA CHAMPIONSHIPS

Loving our spouse takes conscious effort, but many couples today get swept up in the chaos of life and let love fall by the wayside. We have competitions, recitals, deadlines, and schedules that are constantly vying for our attention. We have a barrage of information, tweets, and texts always ready for our review. We have sports updates, advertisements everywhere, and endless pressures to succeed. How can we remember to show love to our spouse daily when there are days we hardly see each other?

For parents, the battle for time is even more difficult. Parenting has become busier than ever before as moms and dads seek to ensure their child has rock-solid self-esteem and a leg up on the competition. We enroll our three-year-olds in sports and music and camps, hoping that they can keep up with the neighbor kid, who is doing even more. We desperately want our kids to have every advantage, and we want them to know we love them and would do anything for them. That might be fine for the kids (for the most part). It's not so good for marriage. Studies show that we spend far more time with our kids today than parents of previous generations, which leaves significantly less time to devote to our marriages. What do kids say when researchers ask what they want? They want parents who are happier and less stressed out!

I can relate to the transformation from loving and attentive newlywed to distracted, busy parent. Scott and I met seventeen years ago at a college barbecue. A mutual friend introduced us, and we couldn't be separated the rest of the evening. In the months that followed, I found myself falling hard. We talked until the wee hours of the morning, he brought roses and wrote poems, we dated, we danced. The whole thing was as natural and effortless as breathing—but substantially more exciting. Nine months later, with a ring on my finger, we began debating an August or December wedding. The only point in the December column was Christmas lights, so we started planning for summer.

The wedding was picture perfect, even with the rain that poured down on us. Everyone else ran from tree to tree trying to stay sheltered as we walked around for our photos. We couldn't care less that we were getting soaked. In fact, I'm not sure we even noticed. My cheeks hurt from smiling at the end of the day. This was my ideal life partner, and our life together was going to be all roses and sunshine.

As newlyweds adjusting to our new life, we were still as happy as ever. No one else competed for our attention at home, and our only real responsibilities were to do well in our college courses and earn enough to pay for our 600-square-foot apartment and meals for two. We walked to school together, took classes together, shopped together, ate together, read books together, and played together. Showing our love every day in small and meaningful ways was easy.

Fast-forward a decade and then some. Things are a little different now. Responsibilities are many, and time is scarce. Between us, we have four beautiful kids (ages two to eleven), a lovely home and two-car garage (attached with a mortgage and monthly car payments), a new business (with all the added excitement and stress that comes with that), church responsibilities, volunteer time at school, grocery shopping, daily meals and dishes for six, soccer games, playdates, dance class, piano practice, and homework. It probably goes without saying that the number of love sonnets I receive has reduced dramatically.

Some days, we don't see each other for more than ten minutes as we both race in different directions. He's out to the office and the gym. I'm up to exercise (on a good day), write, make breakfast, and get kids going. He's working hard at the office. I'm working hard at home cleaning, cooking, carpooling, shopping, washing, folding, ironing, and finding moments to sit down and play with the kids. It's a gift to raise a family with the partner that I love; I wouldn't trade it or go back for anything.

Here's the tricky part: showing our love to each other now takes more effort and deliberate attention than it used to. Much more. We must be doing something right. We still often get what we affectionately refer to as "tingles" when we see each other at the end of the day. And it's not entirely a matter of luck or even due to the fact that we both are fairly cheerful people. I can say that we are still best friends and more in love now than on the day we married. Partly, that's because we focus on loving each other in little ways every day.

It takes attention, and in our modern day, our attention is stretched super thin. According to Dr. Edward Hallowell, a teacher at Harvard

Medical School for more than twenty years and the director of the Hallowell Centers for Cognitive and Emotional Health:

> If you don't have time to ponder and wonder, if you don't have time to approach and avoid and put your heart into it, then love will falter here, not because you are a mismatch but because you have not created sufficient focus for love to grow. Attention given and received in proper measure over time, a recipe that varies from couple to couple, leads to a deeper interest in and a greater knowledge of the other person, which constitutes understanding and empathy. Mutual empathy creates a connection. It is impossible to overestimate the power of connection at its strongest. It drives life. But it cannot develop if people are unable to sustain attention over time. Such a mundane obstacle—distraction—ruins millions of potentially intimate relationships in our modern age.

Many couples end the honeymoon stage of their marriage and become so focused on their own paths that they forget one simple thing: their relationship needs tending. In the romantic comedy *How to Lose a Guy in Ten Days*, writer Andie Anderson is assigned to write an article on what women do to drive men away. So she finds someone to date. One thing Andie does in her attempt to get her new guy to throw in the towel is deliver a "love fern." Andie dramatically explains to Ben that the fern symbolizes their love and that he must care for the little plant like he cares for their relationship. Later, Andie pretends to be horrified when she finds the plant withering. "You let our love fern die? Are you going to let us die?" The scene makes me laugh, but I also see some truth in the metaphor. Just as a fern or a garden needs daily attention, so does a marriage.

If you're like my husband, and you love to exercise and be physically fit, here's another analogy for you: Our bodies need regular exercise to stay healthy and to feel good. If we start to ignore the needs of our bodies, we may find ourselves with a little flab around the edges. We might start to feel more tired and run-down. We might not be able to do the same hikes or play the same sports that we once did. If we want to help our bodies feel and look their best, we must take care of them regularly. The same thing goes for love—daily doses keep the feelings strong.

Here's one last image: Picture the love in your relationship as a fire. The fire was easily lit with the sparks of falling in love. At first, the fire is hot and big and bright. For a while, the flames will continue on their own. Eventually, if the fire is ignored, the flames will become smaller and smaller, and go out. In marriage, simple, everyday acts of love and kindness add more logs on the fire. The more logs, the better, and the longer the fire burns, the deeper and hotter the coals in the fire become. With time, the love from a long-burning fire is far more fulfilling than it was when those flames were first sparked. That is the blessing of marriage.

A marriage needs everyday effort if it's going to thrive. It's not the take-a-couple's-trip-once-a-year kind of effort (though I'm definitely a fan of getting away every once in a while). Simple, deliberate acts will do. Something as easy as a love note, a genuinely happy greeting at the door, an expression of encouragement, or a foot rub after a long day will go a long way to show love to our spouse. As marriage researchers Dr. Carol Bruess and Anna Kudak put it, "even though small acts of affection might seem insignificant, the accumulation can result in something significant indeed." Those loving and intentional connections keep the romantic flames alive. It all starts with something as simple as your thoughts.

TWO-MINUTE ACTION STEPS

(COMPLETE ONCE AND REPEAT OFTEN):

Remind yourself every day that the little things, done consistently, make a big impact.

Think about the ways you can create a positive environment for your relationship. Every day for the coming week, think about one way you can have a happy impact on your spouse.

Think about the little things your spouse has done for you that made you feel loved. Write down one thing that meant a lot to you, even if it may have seemed simple at the time.

Chapter 3

What Were You Thinking?
It's All about Perspective

As a single footstep will not make a path on the earth, so a single thought will not make a pathway in the mind. To make a deep physical path, we walk again and again. To make a deep mental path, we must think over and over the kind of thoughts we wish to dominate our lives.

—Henry David Thoreau,
AMERICAN AUTHOR AND TRANSCENDENTALIST

A documentary I recently watched called *Happy* seeks to explain what gives people joy in different parts of the world. The documentary opens with a rickshaw driver in India. By the definition of most Americans, this man has a pretty rough life. He pulls people around on his little cart all day, in hot, cold, or rainy weather. He lives in a small shack with plastic walls. But when this man told his perspective, I was astonished to hear that, more than anything, he feels blessed. As he explained, "Even if my clothes get soaked in the rain, I know they will dry when I run with a passenger. My home is good. One side is open, and the air flows nicely. A plastic tarp covers the exterior, but one side has a window. During the monsoon, we have some trouble with rain blowing inside [the home]. Other than this, we live well." Then he shared how wonderful it feels to have his son waiting to greet him when he comes home. "When he calls out for me, 'Baba!' I am full of joy." This Indian rickshaw driver, who lives in the slums, could easily have said, "Actually, I'm pretty miserable most of the day, and I can't believe my family has to live here. What do I have to be happy about?" But he didn't. He looked at his life with a lens that captured the good.

What Lens Are You Using?

One key factor that affects our ability to love our spouse is the lens we choose to look through. We always have a choice in how we view a situation. If we choose to use a lens that narrows in on our spouse's faults and flaws, then it's going to be a lot harder to feel love and gratitude. On the other hand, if we choose to see the best in our spouse, then affectionate feelings come more easily.

One Saturday, two of our kids had soccer games early in the morning. Sometimes getting four kids under the age of twelve ready in the morning goes smoothly. Most of the time, it does not. This Saturday was fairly typical. As I recall, someone was refusing to brush her hair, someone was missing shin guards, and someone else was begging for pancakes. Meanwhile, Scott was at the gym. Scott loves the gym, using that time as a stress reliever and an enjoyable hobby. He had been especially stressed this particular Saturday since he had just started a business and had been working long hours. He had checked in with me about going to the gym before the soccer game, but our understanding was that he would be home in time to head to the game together. At ten minutes to nine—crunch time—he wasn't home.

I had two ways of looking at this situation. I could let the stress get to me and could huff and puff and ask, "Where in the world is Scott? Why don't I get to go to the gym and have some personal time? I'm with these kids all day!" Or I could use the alternative lens: "I am so glad that Scott is getting some time to himself and working off some of that stress. He needs it." Here are the two text messages I considered sending when it was time to load up: "Where are you? It's time to leave for soccer!" or "Hi, hon. I hope you're having fun. We're heading to soccer. Join us when you can."

I'm not going to say this was or always is an easy choice. I'm also not going to say I always make the right choice. But, luckily, on this occasion I used the better lens, and Scott was grateful. He called just as we were leaving to thank me for being so understanding. Then he met us at the soccer game just a few minutes late. My choice allowed me to have a loving, empathic view of my husband, who has his own needs. It also allowed him to feel my love. And guess what? Choosing that lens took less than two minutes.

My father-in-law explained it well when he shared with me one of the secrets of his parents' love. He said his mother and father were different in a lot of ways. His father, Ron, was very organized and liked things a certain way. Ron's wife, Claire, was vivacious and creative. Sometimes the home was a little chaotic. Ron had a choice of how he could handle the differences between them. According to my father-in-law, "He knew that her style was different. Sure, everything wasn't as structured as he might have liked. But he loved so many things about her, and he chose to focus on that."

Ask yourself: are you your spouse's biggest critic or his biggest fan? Are you focused on her faults or the things that you love? Do you want to think about the dirty socks that can't seem to make it into the hamper or about the fun wrestling match your husband had with the kids on the floor when he got home from work? Do you see more clearly the rather lengthy honey-do list your wife gives you every Saturday on your day off or how she always makes such delightful dinners for the family?

Having good feelings toward your spouse starts with what you choose to see. Positive feelings can make all the difference in whether you are motivated to show your love and affection. As Dr. Gottman puts it, "Our research has shown that feelings of fondness and admiration are the perfect antidotes to contempt," which he defines as the biggest threat to a happy marriage. He continues: "When couples make a full, conscious effort to notice things they like about each other's personalities and character, and to express that fondness right out loud, their relationships typically improve."

Focusing on Strengths

So how do you know what to focus on? Start by looking at the day-to-day things your spouse does (and tries to do) for you and your family. Does he go to work every day? Does she drive the kids where they need to be? Does he tell you that you look nice when you go out on a date? Is she smart? Does he tell great bedtime stories? Does she work hard to stay active and healthy? Does he make a great meatloaf? The possibilities are endless. Everyone has something good they can offer. Don't think about what's not happening. As Carol Bruess and Anna Kudak write in their book *What Happy Couples Do*, "The work of marriage happens in the everyday moments. The how-was-your-day conversation. The cup of coffee. The medicine. The donut hole. The most mundane occurrences of our lives . . . make sure you're not missing those moments by thinking only about what could be. Should be. Ought to be. Once was."

Next, consider what you love about your spouse as a person. For years, psychologists who studied human behavior mostly focused on the bad—why are people depressed? Repressed? Oppressed? Miserable? Only recently have scientists started looking for what makes people happy and what helps them find joy in their relationships. One of the pioneers in happiness research is Dr. Martin Seligman, author of *Authentic Happiness* and *Learned Optimism*. Dr. Seligman writes about how every person has a set of signature strengths. Among these strengths are wisdom, curiosity and interest in the world, originality, emotional intelligence, perseverance, open-mindedness, courage, kindness, the ability to love others, leadership, temperance, self-control, appreciation of beauty, gratitude, hope, spirituality, forgiveness, humor, and enthusiasm.

Your spouse's signature strengths probably played a role when you were first falling in love. For me, I fell in love with Scott's bright mind and zest for life. I had never met someone who made everything seem so interesting, and his enthusiasm brought out the best in me. Consider your spouse. What attracted you to each other in the first place? What do you love? In marriage, living in such close quarters, it's easy to let the things we once fell in love with start to become tiring or even bothersome. But focusing on the downside can easily disconnect a couple and create negativity in the space between you. If we are regularly looking at the bad stuff, we won't be able to see the good. As Dr. Gottman has said, "By simply reminding yourself of your spouse's positive qualities—even as you grapple with each other's flaws—you can prevent a happy marriage from deteriorating."

I'm not saying you should avoid all problems and never bring up issues with your spouse when you have a genuine concern. Having open communication is incredibly important, and problems need to be addressed. (I cover this topic more in Chapter 8.) Simply put, choosing to see your spouse's strengths will help you feel the love that will strengthen your marriage.

Self-fulfilling Prophecy

One of the perks of having a positive view of your spouse is that it can actually impact them for the better. We all want to be our best, and that is easier to do when we know someone believes in us. According to Dr. Seligman, "The ideal self is the image we hold of the very best we are capable of, our highest strengths realized and active. When we feel that we are living up to the ideals that we hold most dearly, we are gratified, and exercising these strengths produces more gratification. When our partner sees this as well, we feel validated, and we work harder not to disappoint our partner's faith in us."

The concept of the self-fulfilling prophecy was demonstrated in a study of teachers in the 1960s. Some teachers were told they had gifted students, while other teachers were told they had average students. In fact, the students had all been randomly assigned. No group of students was more gifted than another. During the study, teachers treated their students differently according to their expectations. The teachers who thought their students were the best and the brightest expected as much. They interacted with their students in a way that made the students believe in themselves. At the end of the study, the students whose teachers thought they were smarter actually performed better than the other students. Belief, the researchers concluded, encourages change, for better or worse.

The same power is possible in marriage. The self-fulfilling prophecy says that when someone believes we are a certain way, we work harder to actually be that way. If we choose to see great possibilities, our spouse is more likely to fulfill our expectations.

Dr. Frank Gunzburg, who has counseled married couples for more than thirty years, puts it this way: "How you think about your spouse, and what you think about your spouse, will determine your feelings and actions. Expect to enjoy each other and you're more likely to." In other words, your expectations affect the way you interact with your spouse, and the way you interact with your spouse can change everything.

If I know Scott sees the best in me, I feel that, and I work harder not to let him down. I wouldn't be writing this book right now if Scott didn't believe in me. He has regularly said to me that he loves this project and loves reading what I've written. That helps motivate me to work hard and give it my best effort. Of course, he couldn't tell me he believes in me if he didn't first choose the lens that says, "My wife is wonderful and is working on something important. She can do this." He could very well have said, "This is a far-fetched dream, and she could probably spend her time better elsewhere." Because he chose to believe in me, he was motivated to share that love, which, in turn, motivated me. Our beliefs have an impact.

Here's one caveat: don't be disappointed when your spouse turns out to be only human. I remember on our first Valentine's Day as husband and wife, I expected roses or chocolates . . . and got nothing. He thought our dinner out was celebration enough (and it should have been). There is something to be said for keeping expectations realistic. My friend Sarah pointed out just how important this has been in her marriage. She and her husband committed to each other, for better or worse. "Because we entered marriage without a parachute," she said, "we have always been grateful for the little things that we did not expect. When I pack Clint a lunch, he considers it a gift. When he does the dishes, I am grateful. I have never expected roses on Mother's Day, and have rarely gotten them. But when he does buy them, it is magical."

So how do you see all the amazing possibilities in your spouse without ending up disappointed? That's the balance. Hope for the best, believe the best, choose to see the best, and keep realistic expectations.. Then, instead of "Well, it's about time," you can really enjoy those moments you believed in all along.

Assuming the Best

Occasionally in marriage, we become frustrated with something our spouse has said or done. That's part of the deal. Two people who are together so often—needing each other but also needing their own space—are bound to experience friction. Different perspectives, different tastes, and different personalities blend into one shared life. Practically everything we do affects our spouse in some way. It becomes all too easy to jump to conclusions.

Early on in our marriage, Scott and I enjoyed watching movies on the couch together in the evening. After big days of work and school, we were usually pretty exhausted. While I had a fairly easy time staying awake, Scott would almost always fall asleep on the couch. I didn't mind that part so much. What I did mind was the fact that he would stay asleep. On the couch. All night long. I would nudge him and tell him the show was over, softly at first. Then I moved to practically bouncing on the poor man. Nothing. He wouldn't budge. This drove me crazy! So I stormed off to bed thinking how awful it was that my husband was staying on the couch and I was sleeping alone in our bed. That sleeping arrangement was supposed to be for couples in trouble, right? I let my thoughts wander to how stubborn it was of Scott to keep lying on that couch rather than simply walking to our room to be with me.

Of course, I was missing the simple fact that Scott is just a deep sleeper. I wasted so much energy on that couch. I could have very easily just laughed and said, "Wow, he is such a deep sleeper! Guess I get more legroom tonight!" Luckily, sometime between then and now, I grew up a little. We also got a laptop to watch movies in bed.

Marriage researchers have studied how couples handle frustrating behaviors. In one study of fifty-four newlywed couples, tracked over four years, researchers watched whether spouses explained the behavior with accusations about their partner or whether they assumed the best about their partner, coming up with some reasonable explanation. An accusation for laundry left on the couch is "He is so lazy." A reasonable explanation is "He must have been in a hurry." Sixteen of the couples divorced or separated during the study. Researchers found that using a positive, reasonable explanation for behavior in frustrating moments had an impact on marriage satisfaction. The more positive the explanations of behavior were, the more likely the couple was to stay together.

The real-world implication? When your spouse does something you don't like, try to find a temporary explanation (like a tough work week) rather than attributing it to character flaws (like selfishness, stubbornness, or laziness). *He was tired* as opposed to *he's selfish. She has been pent up with the kids and is a little stressed* rather than *she is an uptight person.* Assuming the best in your spouse goes a long way for the feelings of love in marriage. How long does it take? Not more than a couple of minutes.

Gratitude

Another quick and meaningful question to ask yourself is this: "Am I focused on how grateful I am that my spouse does X rather than how crazy it drives me that he does Y?" An attitude of gratitude sets the emotional stage for a couple to be willing, ready, and excited to love and nurture one another.

Science confirms the benefits of grateful thoughts. When we are able to focus on what we are grateful for, we are stronger emotionally and are better able to connect with others than when we focus on what we don't have. According to Dr. Robert Emmons, a psychology professor at UC Davis, people who regularly think about the things they are grateful for are more likely to achieve goals, are more optimistic, energized, and empathic, feel more connected to others, and have better personal relationships. Gratitude journaling also makes a difference for helping people feel happy. In a two-week study, college students who wrote in a gratitude journal every night were happier after the study than students who didn't. Consider what that means for marriage. Just taking a few minutes to think about and even write down what we are grateful for can affect our mood and outlook on everything, causing us to be happier and more satisfied with our spouse.

I find that if I ever start to feel frustrated about something my spouse is doing, making a quick mental shift to gratitude makes a huge difference. It's easy to judge each other. It can be harder to consciously focus on gratitude. But I would much rather think about how grateful I am that Scott went to work all day to provide for our family than simmer over why he's locked in the bathroom with his iPad when it's time to get the kids ready for bed. If I take a step back, I'd remember that he was right there helping with bedtime the last two nights and probably just needs some time to himself. And if I wait just a bit longer, I will see him come out refreshed and ready to make them giggle with "Paul the tickling polar bear". Letting a little gripe in a moment override my thoughts about what I love is really just creating an unnecessary wedge between us.

Your Happiness Is My Happiness

One of the greatest tools for creating a loving connection with your spouse is genuinely wanting their happiness more than your own. This may take years to figure out. If I truly want Scott's happiness more than my own, and he isn't feeling well after a dinner party that has left us with a kitchen full of dishes, I will gladly send him to bed. If he wants my happiness more than his own, when he knows I need a break, he will send me off for a run on a Saturday morning, even with four small kids to care for at home. If I want his happiness, I will be ready to genuinely celebrate his successes and genuinely mourn for his sorrows. This is a magical part of being loving partners. We are there for each other, and we give without expecting anything in return.

Consider how you feel about your partner's happiness. Do you genuinely care about your spouse's physical and emotional well-being? Is your happiness connected to your spouse's? This frame of mind is a choice. We can choose to want all the best for our spouse. We must remember that our own well-being is connected to our spouse's. If we can remember that, then we can truly love and give our spouse what he or she needs most.

Here's what it all comes down to: our thoughts affect our marriage. It's not always easy, but working to focus every day on the positives will benefit our relationship. Just like the rickshaw driver in India could say he was a blessed man, even in his humble circumstances, we too can choose to see the best in our spouse. We can choose gratitude. We can desire our spouse's happiness above our own. That perspective will strengthen our love, tighten our bond, and motivate our partner to be his or her best self. Only then will we be ready to genuinely give our love every day through our words and deeds.

Two-Minute Action Steps

(COMPLETE ONCE AND REPEAT OFTEN):

Think about or write down what you love about your spouse and what you are grateful for.

Consider why you fell in love with your spouse. Write down three of your spouse's signature strengths.

With the concept of self-fulfilling prophecy in mind, think about what hopes you have for your spouse. What do you believe he or she is capable of?

The next time your spouse does something that frustrates you, come up with a reasonable, temporary explanation (such as "He must have been tired" or "She must have had a stressful day") rather than a character accusation.

Remind yourself that you want your spouse's happiness as much as your own and that your happiness is inextricably linked to your spouse's.

Chapter 4

Could You Repeat That?
The Power of Loving Words

*Words—so innocent and powerless as they
are, as standing in a dictionary, how potent for
good and evil they become in the hands of one
who knows how to combine them.*

—Nathaniel Hawthorne, AMERICAN NOVELIST

The words we use to convey our love, appreciation, and respect are key ingredients in a fulfilling partnership. Our words have the power to cause irreparable harm, but they also hold the power to lift, motivate, strengthen, and renew. They can push us apart, or they can intimately connect us. The words we use are so important that a relationship can thrive or fail depending on how they are used. For a happy and rewarding marriage, couples must find ways to connect regularly through loving words, gratitude, admiration, questions, compliments, and even laughter.

Whether the words we use with our spouse come face to face, over the phone, in a letter, via text, or on a computer screen, they make a difference. Like the words written by my husband on that little white note in my finances folder, a simple sentence can turn any dreary situation upside down. This chapter captures a few combinations of letters that, though seemingly small on a page, can make a profound impact with the person you love most. Try a few of these out with your spouse (but be sincere, of course!). I bet you'll be surprised at what a simple sentence can do.

"I love you."

Everyone needs to know they are loved. Maybe you've heard it a thousand times in your years of marriage. Maybe you haven't heard it for months. This much is true for everyone: hearing "I love you" today, in this moment, makes a difference. It conveys the message that even after all the ups and downs and changes in life, your spouse *still* loves you.

One of my favorite romantic comedies is *The Mirror Has Two Faces*. In this movie, a mathematics professor at Columbia named Gregory decides that romance ruins relationships because once the sparks die between two people, there is nothing left to connect them. He decides to seek a companion with common interests and mutual respect but opts to leave romantic love behind. Rose, another professor, agrees to the arrangement, even though she secretly wants passion and romance. After they marry, Rose falls in love with Gregory and keeps hoping he will fall for her in return. Losing hope, Rose realizes she is unhappy without the open expression of love in her life. Her explanation is that maybe romantic love is crazy, but "I want mess and chaos, and I want someone to go crazy out of his mind for me. I want to feel passion and heat and sweat and madness, and I want Valentines and cupids and all the rest of that crap. I want it all." She walks out, leaving him confused and frustrated that his perfect marriage equation wasn't working out.

In her absence, Gregory realizes that he has unintentionally fallen desperately in love with Rose and is going crazy without her. Gregory goes to her apartment at dawn shouting at her window until she comes down to the street to meet him. He explains how sorry he is and, as he holds her close, he says those seemingly simple words: "I love you." This statement leaves her melting in his arms after waiting so long to hear it. Someone whom she loved so much had finally expressed his love in return.

Yes, this is fiction, but as a viewer, the scene brings out real emotions because I understand how wonderful it is to know that I am loved. I remember the first time Scott told me he loved me. We were lying in a field near the airport watching the planes fly in overhead. We had been dating for a few months, gradually growing fonder of each other and spending more time together. When he said those little words, the effect was electric, and I told him I had fallen in love, too. I often think to myself, *Isn't it spectacular, and rather miraculous, that one person can begin to love someone who loves him or her in return?*

The first time we say "I love you" is a significant marker in our relationship. It bridges the gap between a casual romantic fling or mutual friendship and a caring, intimate partnership. These aren't words you say to just anyone. Outside of family and maybe our closest friends, these words are reserved for someone incredibly unique and special. Once we marry, in all likelihood, we say these words romantically to one person only—the person to whom we have committed our whole heart and soul.

When should we express our love? Scott and I are in the habit of saying "I love you" often, including when we part at the beginning of the day and when we reunite. We also say it when we are getting off the phone. Those are wonderful moments to connect and communicate our affection. But when it feels the most meaningful is when it is unexpected and out of routine. For example, the other morning, Scott and I were lying in bed and he rolled over to look at me and say, "I love you." It touched me because, in that moment, he knew I wasn't expecting it. He just wanted to say it because he felt it.

Don't assume that because you said it yesterday or last week or last year that your spouse knows how you feel. Saying "I love you" is an important validation, even when we've said it a thousand times before. These simple words convey powerful messages, such as "I am *still* glad I'm here with you," "I *still* think you are wonderful," and "I would *still* do anything for you." The words are so simple yet so profoundly connecting for two partners who truly care. Say it often, when it is expected and when it isn't. Consider it more fuel on your romantic fire.

"I am grateful for you."

In marriage, our life is constantly and inextricably linked with our spouse. So much of what we do impacts each other. We want to know that what we do is noticed and makes a difference.

My brother-in-law expressed to me how important it is for him to know that his wife appreciates him. "It makes such a difference," he said. "Sometimes when I wake up in the morning, I don't really feel like going to work. I mean, I enjoy it once I get there, but there are days when it's hard to go. When my wife tells me that she is so grateful for all I do for our family, it makes me feel great and helps me stay motivated." He went on to share that, even with the smaller things, hearing her words of gratitude makes a difference. "If I've mowed the lawn or something like that, and she was expecting something else, she might not express her appreciation. It almost makes me feel like I wish I had done something else rather than mow the lawn. But when she notices and thanks me for my efforts, I feel loved and appreciated. Everything I do is to make her happy, and I want to know she notices."

My friend Brian expressed a similar feeling about his wife's expression of gratitude. "I work mainly to support her and our future," he said. "If I was single, I would probably do something a little more 'fun,' so when she is grateful and expresses her appreciation for my success, it truly is a way I feel understood for all my hard work."

For a stay-at-home spouse helping four kids almost constantly throughout the day, "thank-yous" come few and far between. Sometimes my kids are good at remembering, but more often than not, I'm reminding them to say "thank you" when I've helped them with something. That doesn't have quite the same effect as when they spontaneously express their appreciation for my efforts. Most days, the only unprompted appreciation and acknowledgment in my day comes from my spouse. Considering how important it is for a person to feel acknowledged, that's a lot of pressure for Scott! Luckily, he's extremely good at thanking me for the little things like clean sheets on the bed, a mowed lawn, or a warm meal. Those words of gratitude make a huge difference for me and help me feel his love.

What a simple thing—to express our gratitude for each other, even for the things each person is committed to doing anyway. I remember several times when I've thanked Scott for going to work, something I know he would do regardless of my expressions. But my words make a difference. He always seems genuinely grateful to hear them. He often responds with, "Thank you for saying that." Many nights at the dinner table, after someone has thanked me for the meal, I try to help the kids remember that Dad worked hard, too. Then they always say, "Thanks, Daddy, for going to work." We all want to be recognized for our efforts.

Notice the little things your spouse does around the house, with the kids, or at work. Say "thank you" as often as you notice something good your spouse has done for you or your family. Showing gratitude for those things will generate positive connections and loving feelings.

"I admire you."

Perhaps just as important as expressing words of love is making sure your spouse knows that you admire and respect who they are. According to radio personality Dr. Laura Schlessinger, feeling respected is particularly important for men, but I can safely say women want that respect, too. Our concept of ourselves stems, to a great degree, from the way we think others see us. This starts in childhood and continues through our whole lives. As American sociologist Robert Bierstedt put it, "The way we imagine ourselves to appear to another person is an essential element in our conception of ourselves. In other words, 'I am not what I think I am, and I am not what you think I am. I am what I think you think I am.'" That may seem a bit extreme, especially considering that people can triumph over the worst expectations. Still, our concept of self is connected to how we think others see us, especially the one person who knows us best of all. If we don't think our spouse respects and admires the person we are, hearing "I love you" won't have the power it should.

How do we let our spouse know we admire and respect him or her? We can express this partly through our actions, and, also, importantly, through our words. We must share what we admire and enjoy about our spouse. I have a close friend who has struggled on and off for years in her marriage. When I told her about this project, the first thing she said to me was, "A flower or a love note means very little if I don't feel my spouse respects me as a person or if he has been critical of how I do things. I need to know he respects who I am before anything."

Scott's mom, Kerry, has told me how important it is to know that her spouse admires and respects her. "Even though he knows all my flaws and idiosyncrasies," she explained, "I know he admires me. He even says kind things about me to our friends and neighbors, which shows me that he will always be on my side. His expressions of respect over time have built a trust. I know how he sees me, and that makes me feel loved." There is security in knowing our spouse admires and sees the best in us, everywhere they go.

Once at a family gathering, Kerry got up for a family presentation in which she shared all the things that she and her husband loved about their children. Although the two parents prepared together, Kerry did the talking. At the end, she asked if her husband, Mark, wanted to say anything. He summed up his feelings in a sentence or two, and then he teased his wife for talking so much. Later, he told her, "I hope you know that I love how you have so many wonderful words to share. I'm not the same way, but I'm glad that's a strength for you." In that instance, he validated her and let her know he sees the best in her. She hadn't thought twice to be offended by his teasing because, as she put it, "I have that confidence in knowing how he really feels about me. We have that trust."

In the corporate world, measures are typically in place to recognize and praise employees who have excelled. When I was working at a public relations firm, we were promoted and recognized at weekly meetings when we had performed well. I remember how good that "Somebody thinks I am great at what I do!" acknowledgment felt. It was a feeling we could soak up for a while. If recognition and praise can affect us so much in our day job, just imagine what it can do in our marriage.

For me, the little things Scott does to show his respect mean a lot. I know he admires me and the way I go about my life, even if there are days when all I've done is change dirty diapers and scrub dirty toilets. Formal recognition isn't part of the stay-at-home-mom position. I would argue that I work harder now than I ever did at a day job before having kids. My day is filled with helping the kids get ready, carpooling, doing laundry, shopping, ironing, cleaning bathrooms, vacuuming, paying bills, doing yard work, helping with homework and piano, cooking meals, and taking moments to teach and play with our kids. It's not like I really want Scott to say, "Wow, you did such a nice job cleaning those dishes," although I do like knowing that he noticed. What means more to me is hearing Scott tell me "You are so good with our kids. I trust your style with them so much" or "I don't know how you do everything you do in a day. You're amazing."

Providers feel great too when they know their spouse is proud of their efforts out in the world, even with all the recognition that comes with an office environment. My brother-in-law, with his busy investment banking career, told me, "I think it's great when my wife says she's proud of me. That shows she appreciates me and the effort I put in. I like knowing she thinks I represent her well and that she values the effort I make in doing good things for our family and for the world." The same thing holds true whether the husband, the wife, or both spouses are working outside the home—acknowledging the effort is what matters.

Admiring your spouse is as easy as finding things you like, but its importance can't be overstated. As Dr. Gottman puts it, "Fondness and admiration are two of the most crucial elements in a rewarding and long-lasting romance." Think about what your spouse does every day. Think back on your spouse's signature strengths discussed previously. What personality traits do you appreciate? What is your spouse good at? Is it how she makes your kids laugh? Is it his gardening skills? Is she great at her job? Is he the best Little League coach in town? Is she great at expressing herself?

Remember, you are your spouse's biggest fan. Even if there is a gap between your perception and reality, research shows that can be a good thing for marriages. Maybe technically your spouse isn't the world's best bedtime story teller, like you've said for years (in fact, there's a guy in Singapore that sports full costumes and accents every night). So what? It's what *you* think of your spouse that matters. Let yourself see the best in your partner. Then let your spouse know.

"I like the way you . . ."

Giving a compliment is a simple way to let your spouse know "I like something about you." It is an opportunity to point out something positive in the moment, whether that's how nice she looks tonight, what a great meal he prepared for breakfast, or her flattering new haircut. Giving genuine compliments regularly is a quick and easy way to build feelings of affection in the space between you.

Scott recently explained to me how much it means to him when I compliment him. He said, "The other morning, you told me I'm handsome. It caught me off guard. It feels good to know you think so. And what's great is that it's not something just there for that moment. It lingers. I thought about it the next day when I was getting ready. 'She thinks I'm handsome.' That's fun."

My friend Brian said something similar when I asked him how he felt loved in his marriage. He said, "Just the other day, at random, we were driving in the car, and she tells me that she is so proud of me, loves me so much, how attractive I am, and how generous, thoughtful, kind, and attentive I am to her needs. She simply told me how much I mean to her, how happy she is to be married to me, and how lucky she is. There was no guessing on how she feels, no reading between the lines, and no hints I have to decipher. I love that."

Opportunities to compliment your spouse are endless. Notice details like a new haircut, a new dress, a well-cooked meal, a nicely mowed lawn, a new tie, or even a clean sink. For me, I love it when Scott tells me I look nice or that he thinks I'm good with the kids. We all naturally feel good when we receive positive attention. Find ways to build those positive feelings by complimenting your spouse. You are the one who knows your spouse best, and it will mean more coming from you than from anyone else.

"A guy walks into a bar . . ."

One of the most enjoyable things about companionship is having someone you can laugh with, someone who can make you smile. Having fun and enjoying your time together is actually one of the most important things you can do for your marriage. As marriage counselor Dr. Jim Burns has said, "Friendship and fun in a marriage are two of the biggest predictors of long-term marital satisfaction." Research even confirms that laughter is healthy for relationships, emotionally and chemically connecting us. When we laugh together, our brains release oxytocin, appropriately dubbed the "love hormone" because it serves as a connecting hormone.

Beyond strengthening our friendship, making each other laugh is also an easy way to show each other we care. I think my sister put it well when she told me one of the biggest ways that she feels loved by her husband is when he makes her laugh. "He's got a great sense of humor, and it feels good when he tells me a joke or does a little silly thing to make me smile," she explained. "It's important to me that we laugh and have fun together because life is really tough sometimes with work, baby, growing our business, etc. It feels good to smile, laugh, and be happy together."

I couldn't agree more. A few weeks ago, I had had a tough day with our kids. It was just one of those days where everyone seemed to need something all day long, and they were having more of a worst-of-enemies than best-of-friends kind of afternoon. My nerves were fried, and Scott could tell. He came over to me and said, "I'm not sure about this, but I think you might like watching this clip." We have often chuckled about how different men and women are when it comes to problems and how sometimes women just want someone to listen to them but their man wants to problem solve. So Scott sat by me on the couch and pulled up a YouTube clip on his phone. In the clip, a woman has a pretend nail coming out of her forehead and is saying "My head really hurts, and my clothes keep getting snagged, and it's so frustrating." Her partner is looking at her, saying, "Well, that's because you have a nail in your forehead." She gets mad at him, saying, "Can't you just listen to me? I just want you to listen." He looks at her a little unsure, like, "But . . ." She stops him and continues to explain how her head hurts and how she just needs someone to listen. He bites his tongue and nods. "Yeah, that must be frustrating."

The clip was so unexpected and made me laugh out loud. That took Scott two minutes to do, but it made me love him so much in that instant because I felt (1) that he cared about my feeling stressed, (2) that he knew me well enough to know what I would find funny, and (3) that he wanted to make me smile.

What a simple thing it is to make each other laugh in life. By telling each other jokes, or at least giving our best attempt to make each other smile, we create more loving feelings. So watch a funny YouTube clip together, tell each other a joke, or as the two PhDs who wrote *Making Marriage Simple* did, wear Groucho Marx glasses during dinner and see what happens. The point is, one of the most enjoyable parts of a friendship is making each other laugh. Keep it interesting, laugh, and have fun together. You will add positive connections to the space between you in no time.

"How was your day?"

Simply having our spouse ask about our thoughts and opinions or about our experiences, no matter how routine, communicates love and concern. Asking someone to share his or her experiences and feelings says, "I care and want to know about you." Get to know each other. Don't assume because you knew each other last month, last year, or when you got married that there is nothing new to know. As human beings, we are constantly learning, growing, changing, and experiencing. Find out what your spouse is going through. Ask about what happened during your spouse's day and be ready to listen with sincere interest. Ask about her thoughts and opinions, likes and dislikes, hopes and fears. As Scott explained, "You want to check in because you care. You're interested. That makes me feel that what I do is important to you."

My father-in-law is a busy attorney with plenty of worldly success. You wouldn't think something as simple as "How was your day, dear?" could mean that much to a guy who brokers multi-million-dollar deals. But when I asked him about the little things that mean a lot to him, he said this: "A guy who's been at work all day can come home feeling stressed. To have my wife ask me, sincerely, how my day was and show that she's willing to sit with me and listen to my trials, well, that's huge. Absolutely huge."

Scott's brother, who works at an investment bank in New York, feels the same way. When I asked him how he feels loved by his wife, one of the things he said first was, "I love it when she asks about my day, even though some people might think it's boring or uninteresting. She seems to really be interested, partly because she is interested in me." I can relate. When Scott gets home from work, more often than not, our kids are all over him, and we can hardly get two words in to each other. That chaotic state typically lasts through dinnertime. We laugh about how hard it is to have more than a thirty-second exchange while our kids are awake. They are so excited to share their projects and wrestle and be tickled by Dad. We love that time to connect with our kids.

But at night, after the last child has gotten up to ask for one *last* drink of water and gone back to bed, that's our time. It's so important to me that Scott knows he can't ask me "So what do you want to do?" until we have talked for a little while about our day. I love connecting with him and hearing about what he did. I love having him ask me about my day—not because he knows that's the only gateway to the television show he really wants to watch but because he really wants to know. It doesn't take long to say those simple words: "Tell me about your day." Yet think about what that communicates: "I am interested in you. I care about you. I want to know about you and your experiences."

We had a chance to connect through questions more extensively on a recent date, which was one of the most enjoyable in my memory. It was as simple as bringing a picnic lunch to the park and playing a get-to-know-you game. We picked questions from a marriage book and tried to guess what the other would say about a certain topic. We laughed and we learned. It was so fun to hear how much Scott knows about me. He even learned something new about me—my favorite animal is a white tiger. It's still up for debate whether the answer "cat" should earn the needed points for a tie. Either way, we strengthened the love between us by simply asking questions.

Asking questions about our spouse's opinion also conveys a lot of love. Whether it's what to do about a child, a work problem, a political situation, or a paint color, asking our spouse's opinion shows we care what they think. That's just another way of generating the positive connections that are so important in marriage. As Scott put it, "When you ask for my thoughts on something, that shows I'm an important sounding board to you. You're interested to know what I think, and that feels good. I feel important and appreciated." Ask questions—your spouse will appreciate your interest and feel your love.

Take an opportunity to learn more about your spouse's thoughts, interests, and opinions. Use the following questions for a fun exercise, either on a date or for a few minutes at the end of the day. Choose a question randomly and see if your spouse knows your answer. Then have your spouse do the same. Use this exercise as a fun way to learn new things about your spouse and see what your spouse knows about you.

- What is my favorite color?
- Who is my favorite musician or composer?
- What did I do today?
- What is one of my greatest fears?
- Who is my greatest hero?
- What is one of my three favorite movies?
- Who is my favorite author?
- What are three of my hopes for the future?
- What is my idea of a perfect date?
- Name one of my hobbies.
- What stresses am I facing today?
- What is my favorite song?
- What would be my perfect job?
- Who is my favorite relative outside of our immediate family?
- What is my favorite flower?
- What is my favorite season?
- Name one accomplishment I am proud of.
- What is my favorite meal?
- What goals I am trying to accomplish?
- What was my favorite vacation?

- What is one of my favorite childhood experiences?
- What is my favorite thing to do to relieve stress?
- What is one of my favorite ways to spend a Saturday?
- Name one of my best friends from childhood.
- Name a childhood pet that I had.
- What is one of my favorite magazines?
- What is my favorite holiday?
- What is my favorite TV show?
- Name one thing I worry about.
- What was one of my most embarrassing moments?
- What is my favorite dessert?
- Name one of my favorite restaurants.
- What is my favorite sports team?
- Who are my two closest friends (other than you)?
- What is an event I am looking forward to?
- What was one difficult time in my life?
- Describe what kind of family environment I grew up in.
- Where would I like to be in five years?
- What do I hope to leave behind as a legacy when I die?
- Name three characteristics that I hope others see in me.

When "I" Becomes "Us"

Talking about your partnership as "we" rather than "he (or she) and I" makes a difference in marriage. It sounds like a simple thing, and maybe it is, but whether you describe your partnership as a together team or as two separate individuals really does matter. Marriage researchers who study how couples talk about themselves have found that happy couples use partner pronouns like "we," "us," and "our" when sharing their experiences.

So, if someone asked me about my weekend, I might say "We

went to dinner at our favorite restaurant, and we went to the new Superman movie" rather than "I went to dinner and a movie." It's subtle, but that change can make a difference for your couple connection. As my sister-in-law reminded me, this also applies to times when people want to schedule something with you and your spouse. "It's important that we get each other's buy-in before we commit to something," she said. "We want to be on the same page." That is a principle Scott and I live by. Scott calls it our "unified front." Even if we disagree at first on something like getting together for a family dinner at six or seven o'clock, once we decide, we respond in a unified way, saying, "We would love to come over at 6:30" (not "Well, *he* wanted to come at 6:00, but *I* thought that was too early"). Do you feel the difference? We all have the choice to communicate about our life in a certain way. We can choose to convey a partnership, especially when sharing our history, our experiences, and our plans. Do you see and communicate about your marriage as though you are a team?

On the flip side, at times, using individual pronouns, like "I," is important. When it comes to describing opinions and thoughts unique to your personality, according to psychologist Susan Heitler, using "I" can be refreshing and help keep separate identities intact. No one wants to feel suffocated or that their spouse is taking over their personality. So, saying "We are really excited to get a cat" when one of you feels the opposite can breed frustration rather than connection. As Heitler explains, "The ability to maintain clear boundaries between yourself and others enables you to individuate, to feel legitimate in having your own attitudes, beliefs, and desires, and to feel comfortable letting your partner have attitudes, beliefs, and desires that differ from yours." That keeps marriage connected without being stifling.

Both types of pronouns have a place in marriage. In a nutshell, using "we" is great for sharing experiences, making plans, and creating a team environment, while using "I" allows each person to feel comfortable communicating their own identity and opinions. Pay attention to your pronouns, and use these little words to both strengthen your connection and respect your independence.

"Great job, Honey!"

Marriage science tells us that celebrating good news with our spouse is critical. In fact, research shows that celebrating the good times may be even more important to marital happiness than how we handle the bad times. Think for a moment: the last time your spouse came home with great news, what did you do?

One study shows how your level of enthusiasm for your spouse's good news could be affecting your marriage. To measure the importance of celebrating together, researchers from UCLA and the University of Rochester studied four different ways that spouses typically respond to good news. One type of response is actively constructive. These people shared their excitement and support openly. The second type is passively constructive. These people were supportive of good news or triumphs but in a quiet, backseat kind of way. The third type is actively destructive. These people were not enthusiastic about good news from their spouse and were even discouraging. The fourth type is passively deconstructive. These people were not supportive of positive events and achievements but didn't do anything to discourage them either. In measuring satisfaction, it's fairly easy to guess that people who had spouses that gave deconstructive responses reported lower measures of happiness in their marriages. But interestingly, even people with a passively constructive spouse had lower measures of marital happiness than people with actively constructive spouses.

What does that mean for marriage? The researchers concluded

that when one spouse has good news or achieves something note-worthy, it's not enough to support them quietly. Partners need to openly declare their enthusiasm and excitement with each other to create positive connections. It needs to be so obvious that the spouse with good news clearly feels the support.

This is a fun and rewarding part of our marriage—Scott and I love celebrating each other. I actually painted a special plate before we had kids, and now whenever someone in our family has accom-plished something, that person gets to eat off the "Celebrate Plate." It's so small and easy, and yet, in our family, it means a lot. As Scott said, "I love getting that plate. It's a symbol of how you celebrate me. It shows that my joy is your joy. That's bonding."

For the really important accomplishments, we may do some-thing bigger. For example, when we found out Scott passed the California Bar Exam—the exam you must pass after law school to begin practicing as an attorney—we went out to our favorite restaurant to celebrate. Birthdays and anniversaries are important, too. We go out to dinner, and we commemorate. For my last birth-day, I woke up to balloons around the house. I felt loved indeed. On his birthday four days later, Scott woke up to streamers around our room. Granted, that takes a bit more than two minutes. What really matters is attitude, and that can be conveyed in seconds. Are you excited when your spouse has something to celebrate?

A friend of mine shared with me how important her spouse's enthusiasm for her accomplishments is to her. Shannon is an athlete and personal trainer and loves to participate in events. Recently, she accomplished a goal she's had for seven years to race in LoToJa, a 206-mile bike race across Utah, Idaho, and Wyoming. When she finished the race, her husband was there to celebrate her success. "As I came across the finish line," she said, "he embraced me in tears, trembling, and said, 'You killed it, "best" (that's what we call each other). I can't believe you . . . you killed it. I love you so much!' His whole heart was there. It wasn't this task I was making him do. He wanted to be there. He would be no place else, and I felt that. This kind of honest support doesn't just happen. We've both worked on it our whole marriage."

I felt the love coming through Shannon's words as she wrote to me about how grateful she was for her husband's clear pride and support. For every couple, celebrating each other is important, whether that's passing a test, publishing an article, finishing a race, losing those last five pounds, or just having a birthday. Celebrating shows that our spouse's happiness and success is our own happiness and success. It communicates that we are a team, intertwined with and ever impacted by each other.

"Hey, Pookie."

Do you have words, phrases, nicknames, and inside jokes with your partner that no one else understands? Marriage researchers say that's a good thing. Whether it's a secret phrase that really means "Let's leave the party" or a loving nickname, these codes create a sense of "we-ness." Nicknames and terms of endearment, in particular, are powerful connecters that strengthen the invisible bond between partners. They create a boundary, marking your relationship as exclusive. You have something together that you don't share with anyone else. For Scott and me, if one of us says, "Hey, best friend," the other person always responds with, "Hey, lover." It's a code we don't use with anyone else.

My mom and her husband have nicknames for each other that have evolved over time. They started out calling each other "Honey bunny" which they still do. Recently, I realized that term has evolved to just "Bunny." I had to smile when I heard it because it's so silly and cute at the same time. To them, one word says "I love you so much that I am going to call you by a name that you and I understand is special, and it's just between us."

If you haven't already, create your own personal terms of endearment for each other. They can be commonly used terms—like Honey or Sweetheart—or something goofy backed by a story that only you understand. It doesn't have to make sense to anyone but the two of you. Consider these odd nicknames from real couples: Big Daddy Rabbit, Boobala, Bunnie Mae, Cherry, Corn Chip, Fez, Girdle, Hoki Fish, Moo, Loopy, Peeper, Poochy, Pookey Pie, Rapster, Rotunda, Sneezy, Sparky, Stinker, Sushi, and Zaddy. Whatever it is, make sure it is something that makes you both smile. Unique terms of endearment, if used well, are a simple way to strengthen your couple connection.

Our words have the power to bless or curse. Choose words that will strengthen the loving bond between you. Regularly use words that will help your spouse feel loved, appreciated, and respected. Use words to get to know your spouse better or to make her smile. Show him you care and that you notice the things he does. Whatever you do, be sure to use your words as a force for good in your marriage, and your love will grow.

TWO-MINUTE ACTION STEPS

(COMPLETE ONCE AND REPEAT OFTEN):

Find an unexpected, out-of-routine time to tell your spouse "I love you."

Choose one thing your spouse does that you are grateful for, and let your spouse know.

Think about something you admire about your spouse, and let him or her know.

Give your spouse a compliment.

Say something that will make your spouse smile, whether it's a joke, a funny story, or something silly.

Choose two questions from this chapter that will help you and your spouse get to know each other better—then enjoy the discussion!

Think about how you discuss your shared history. Do you use "we" or "I"? Remember that using couple pronouns like "we" and "us" builds unity.

The next time your spouse tells you good news, openly and enthusiastically celebrate and share in the excitement.

Use a term of endearment with your spouse that is meaningful to just the two of you.

Chapter 5

Taking Action: Little Deeds That Make a Big Difference

Love is not [just] thinking about it;
it is doing it. It is loving.

—**Eric Butterworth,** AMERICAN MINISTER

We make connections with our spouse with every little act of love we give. Over time, these seemingly simple acts keep the affection in our marriage alive and well. Whether it's bringing our spouse his favorite drink, writing her a simple love note, welcoming him with a hug and smile at the door, or playing a love song for her, these small, affectionate gestures make a big difference in the space between us. These are the acts that keep us close.

Create Rituals

Having little rituals that mean something only to the two of you creates a unique bonding experience that lasts over time. They can be simple, even mundane, but these loving rituals, done time and again, are a sure way of reminding two people of what makes them a couple. As Carol Bruess and Anna Kudak have found in their fifteen years of study, happy couples have rituals that are "the heartbeat of your marriage: steady, repeated, often taken for granted." These rituals say something about a couple's unique shared history and interests and, according to research, clearly strengthen the relationship.

For example, consider the wife who one day found a bit of fuzz in her husband's belly button. She pulled it out, teasing him at first. Then she began checking his navel for fuzz every day. She was still doing it ten years later. On days when he didn't have any fuzz, he would put some there for her to find. The daily search-and-rescue effort became so meaningful that she even began collecting the naval fuzz in a little tin. Disgusting? Maybe. But for this couple, the belly-button ritual was a funny and unique way to connect every day. Scott and I have a ritual that we dubbed "the stair hug." Scott is several inches taller than me, but when I'm standing on a step higher than him, my arms fit nicely around his neck. Starting when we were just dating, whenever we would walk up or down stairs together, one of us would stop along the way and say, "Stair hug!" Then we promptly engaged in our favorite embrace. We've done this for years now, outside, inside, at home, on escalators. It's just a simple thing that means something only to us.

Here's another silly ritual that started when we were dating: We name everything Bill. If we see an animal—alive, statue, stuffed, or otherwise—we name it Bill. We joked that we should name our first son William, so we could call him Bill. Recently, on a canoe trip for our thirteenth wedding anniversary, we saw a hawk that seemed to be following us. I turned to Scott and said, "Let's name him Bill." Scott laughed. No one else would have gotten that.

Look for ways to create rituals in your relationship, whether it's searching for fuzz, using a special phrase, being the first to put toothpaste on the other person's toothbrush, rubbing noses before bed, or a unique way of betting who's right. (Scott and I have a habit of betting millions against each other when we disagree. We figure it's safe since it all comes from the same place.) Whatever you do, use these rituals often to strengthen your unique couple connection.

Serve Your Spouse

Finding opportunities to lovingly serve one another, without thought of what you will get in return, is an important ingredient for lasting love. The more we are willing to be selfless and find ways to bring our spouse happiness, the more that selfless love will be returned.

One helpful step in being able to truly serve one another is having a clear understanding of responsibilities. Dating life is so fun and rewarding, partially because while two people are courting, they usually don't have to sort out all the responsibilities of life. No wonder it's so easy to fall in love! Then, once two people marry, move in together, and start going about the stuff of real life—like career, household, and childcare duties—the whole landscape changes. It doesn't have to change for the worse. Research shows that couples are happier when everyone understands who does what. And the rules in today's society are more flexible than ever, so it's up to each couple to decide. Once partners know what their responsibilities are, then they can build loving connections by going above and beyond to lovingly serve their spouse.

My friend Melissa shared with me how her husband's offers to help with her responsibilities makes her feel loved. "Not too long ago, we were getting the kids to bed, and it suddenly dawned on me that I had forgotten to pick up some milk," she said. "I turned to Greg and said, 'After we get the kids in bed, I need to go get some milk.' He said, 'I will go.' I proceeded to tell him that I had forgotten, so I would go. He then said, 'I want to do this. I love you.' It sounds like a little thing, but it wasn't just the offer to run the errand that melted me. It was that he genuinely wanted to do something for me. It was a small thing, but it showed that he loves me."

This is a language of love that scores big points in my book, too. Scott knows that almost nothing thrills me more than seeing him in an apron putting dishes in the dishwasher. Oh, how I love him in that apron. This really isn't a big time commitment. A few minutes and it's over. I usually clean up after dinner while he spends time with the kids because he hasn't seen them all day. But, when he decides to take over dish duty, knowing that he wants to help me means a lot. It communicates, "I care about you and your happiness."

My sister-in-law Lindsay speaks the same language. When I asked her how she feels loved by her husband, she said without missing a beat: "I love it when he helps me around the house or with the kids." That is a common feeling, especially for parents with young kids whose chores and household duties can seem endless. Scott's Aunt Holly described how much she feels loved when her husband is caring for their children. "When he is a part of my life, assisting and helping in the things I do as a mother," she said, "it gives me a deep sense of being cared for."

Even little things that you've never talked about but that still need doing give opportunities to serve. When I asked my neighbor Carol to tell me how she felt loved by her husband, Bob, of fifty-eight years, the first thing she said was, "He cleans my glasses for me every morning. He's thinking of me and tries to make me comfortable." In response, Bob explained how that wasn't something he really thought about. He just enjoys doing it. No wonder his wife felt his love. Scott often does a similar thoughtful act. He knows how much I love orange juice in the morning, and he likes to bring me a glass when I wake up. He is happy to surprise me, without my asking. I love that he knows me and wants to do something for me just because.

It's not hard to find ways to serve your spouse. Scott recently told me of a little good deed from months ago that meant a lot to him. We were in Yellowstone, and our family of five was staying in a little motel room with kids in sleeping bags. Scott was planning to leave early the next morning for a bike ride. I knew it would be dark and everyone would still be sleeping, but I also knew Scott would need something to eat. I prepared a bowl of cereal for him so all he would have to do was pour milk and not worry about getting into all our food bags with three kids sleeping on the floor. I didn't think much of it, and it literally took me two minutes to do. But Scott said, "It was the end of the day, and you were tired. Not only did you bring all the stuff for my favorite breakfast, but you got it ready for me. That meant a lot. You were thinking of me." He was recalling this simple act three months later.

Find a way to serve your spouse. It can be as easy as changing a diaper, picking up some milk, ironing a shirt, turning down the bed, shoveling the walk, making a meal, taking out the trash, or cleaning off glasses—as long as you are doing it *for your spouse*, it is an act of love. These simple acts of service communicate clearly "Your happiness is my happiness." Even doing the jobs you are "supposed" to do is a sign that you care about your spouse's well-being and want to hold up your end of the deal. Whatever it is that your spouse will notice and appreciate, do it, and do it often.

Support Your Spouse

Giving time to do what each person loves individually is key for a healthy relationship. I like how marriage therapists Les and Leslie

Parrott describe the ideal couple in terms of levels of dependency and independency. Couples who have too much independence, who don't connect or rely on each other enough, have what they dub an "H" relationship. If the link is broken, both sides are fine on their own. On the other end of the spectrum is an "A" relationship. If that link is broken, both sides tumble. The ideal is the "M" relationship, in which each side needs the other but they are also independent enough to stand on their own.

One way to keep a healthy sense of independence is to support individual interests and hobbies. When one spouse is able to say, "Please, take some time to do what you love," the relationship is strengthened because (1) the individual is renewed in the opportunity to pursue a personal passion and (2) the person getting the green light to do something for themselves feels the support and affection of their spouse. The simple offer of support is another sign that "Your happiness is my happiness."

Being supportive is more than grudgingly agreeing to a request for personal time. It is, as my friend Shannon put it, "support truly in heart and soul." Shannon, a talented athlete, shared with me how much she appreciates her husband's through-and-through support. "He talks to me about it, glories with me in successes, helps me through down times, and participates with me in some training events, even when it's not his favorite thing to do," she said. "He signs me up online, because he knows I feel guilty about costs. He just does it to save me the grief. I don't even ask him half the time; he just knows the events I love and tells me I'm signed up. He never lets me feel guilty about the time I'm taking to train. I feel his true happiness and joy for me when I do well and his sadness and frustration when I don't."

That kind of loving support for a treasured activity doesn't take long, and it isn't hard if you truly want your spouse's happiness. For me, I appreciate it so much when Scott comes to me and suggests

I take time to go for a run or take a writing day. He said to me recently, "I know you have a deadline coming up, and with all you do with the house and the kids, I know it's hard for you to find time to write. Why don't I hang out with the kids next Saturday while you take a day?" Wow! I felt his love so much with that simple suggestion. He knew me, he knew what I needed, and he made the offer.

Even being supportive of what your spouse needs to do shows love. Scott has expressed to me how important it is to him that I support what he needs to do for his job. "You acknowledge the importance of my role as provider," he said. "You step up without complaint. You ask how you can help. That makes it so much easier to manage the stress of providing for our family."

My neighbors, Bob and Carol, who raised eleven children in their fifty-eight years of marriage, said this kind of support is key to their marital happiness. When I asked Bob what he thought a secret to their success was, he said, "She has always been so supportive of me in all the things I needed to do for church or work. She never complained. She's always been there." In response, she commented how much she appreciated that "he was always so willing to support my interests, too, and give me my own time. That helped a lot." The mutual support had clearly helped them feel each other's love and strengthened their desire to give.

Of course, you can't always be off doing your own thing. But a certain level of healthy, supportive independence is essential. As my mom's husband, Bob, put it: "Sometimes, in marriage, you can just sense when your spouse needs a little space and time to do what they want to do. It takes a fair amount of practice, and you have to be careful not to let your own interests shut out your spouse. But taking some time for your own hobbies is important. Then, when you come back together, you can reconnect and get even closer."

Leave a Love Note

How long does it take you to write three sentences? Less than two minutes, I'll bet. Love notes are one of the easiest things we can do for our spouse, yet they have so much power. Leaving a quick sticky note somewhere your spouse will find it says "Hey! I'm thinking about you right now!" That's fuel for the flames.

Through little love notes, my friend Melissa has helped her husband, Greg, feel her love even when they were far apart. When I asked Greg how he felt loved by his spouse, he said, "I travel quite a bit, often gone for one to two weeks at a time. I left on a two-week business trip one week after our daughter Sarah was born. Melissa was extremely supportive. As I am gone for more than a couple of days, I generally pack a large suitcase. Melissa writes several little notes and hides them in my luggage that I come across every couple of days. These notes express many things and often an appreciation for how hard I work and the sacrifices I make for our family. I really look forward to reading these notes. They consistently remind me that we are team, equally yoked, leading our family together. This makes it easier for me to fulfill one of my roles as a provider, knowing that Melissa is so supportive."

In leaving those notes, Melissa and her husband were brought closer together, even when they were on different continents. It's easy to see the impact such a seemingly small thing has on this husband.

The other night, Scott and I were out to dinner, and we got to talking about love notes. He reminded me of a time when I had stuck a little note in the lunch he was taking to work. He was eating with his colleagues when he found it. He said, "That note was just a little, teeny thing, but it let me know you were thinking about me. It brought our relationship to the forefront and expressed a lot of love. I felt relieved of any other stress from the day in that moment and was reminded of our love. Our relationship is my refuge. Love does that. It's healing. Those little reminders help me refocus on why I am doing all of this." Isn't that amazing? Truly, it was a two-inch square note with two little sentences on it, but to him, in that moment, it meant the world.

Leave your spouse a love note—even, as my creative friend Melinda has done, right there on the toilet paper roll. Put one anywhere you know your spouse will find it. Let him know how much you love, appreciate, or admire him. Let her know you are excited to see her again. Your spouse will appreciate your effort and feel the loving connection in the space between you.

Surprise Your Spouse

Don't we all love receiving gifts? A gift means someone thought of me and picked out something he thought I would like. What a fun and easy way to connect with your spouse—just by bringing home a surprise.

Gary Chapman, author of *The 5 Love Languages*, shares the story of a woman who felt a complete change in her relationship once her husband started coming home with surprises for her. The couple's marriage had been suffering, so Dr. Chapman made a suggestion to the husband: bring home a gift. When he started bringing home little things for his wife like a potted plant, pizza for dinner, or a treat for the kids, it made all the difference. The wife reported, "You wouldn't believe how happy we have been. Our children call us lovebirds now."

My good friend Julie shared with me what little surprises mean to her. "Just today even, Steve wrote me a sweet note, bought me my favorite drink and pack of gum, and hid them in the bathroom where I would eventually see them. It made my day just to know he had been thinking of me." Picking up some gum and a drink at the store on his way home surely didn't take long. It was so simple, and yet this is a way Julie feels love in her marriage.

A little treat can do wonders. When I asked my father-in-law how he feels loved by his wife, he said, "When I come home from work, Mary will often have bought a treat for me, just one cookie, or a brownie, or a chocolate-dipped strawberry. It is not for a birthday or Father's Day or our wedding anniversary. It is simply a surprise treat on a no-nothing day. It means so much because, at the end of a long day, it's fun to come home to a sweet surprise. But, more than that, it says, 'Even when I am not with you, I am loving you.'"

I can relate! Almost without fail, when I ask Scott to pick up something from the store on his way home, he adds a pint of Ben and Jerry's ice cream for me. When he comes home, he slyly pulls out the chosen pint—usually a fun new flavor I haven't tried—and shows me without letting the kids see. It's his way of saying "I got this just for you." It's so sweet and makes me love him even more than I did two minutes before.

It doesn't have to be a sweet surprise. Indeed, if I brought home a pint of ice cream for Scott, he would be confused. (The man hasn't had dessert for fifteen years—but that's a subject for another book.) One thing Scott loves is when I surprise him with a clean car, especially before we go on vacation. Most women—at least most women I know—love flowers. One of Scott's clients asked him recently, "When was the last time you brought home flowers for your wife?" Scott thought it over and then said, "Well, I used to do that more. It's been a while." Then the client told him to go pick up some flowers on the way home. What a wise man! He knew how much something as simple and silly as a flower, which will shortly brown and die, means to a girl. Scott followed his orders (quickly making the client one of my favorites) and has tried to do that more regularly ever since. Think about what your spouse likes, and bring that home as a surprise. You'll be glad you did.

Connect by Phone

Simply giving your spouse a call during the day makes a connection that says "You're on my mind." It feels wonderful to know that someone, my favorite someone, is thinking about me. I love when Scott calls in the middle of the day to say hello, even if he has to leave a message on my phone. I especially like it because I know he's not calling me just because he's bored and has nothing to do (although I would still like being the person he turns to in that scenario). Because he has a busy job, and I know he is constantly running from one thing to the next, the fact that he takes a moment to reach out to me makes me feel important.

My friend Diana, who just celebrated her forty-eighth wedding anniversary, knows those calls are a secret to marital success. As she explained, "Without fail, every time my husband leaves the house to run an errand, almost before the garage door closes, he calls me on his cell phone in the car to tell me, 'Honey, I am missing you already!'" For years, he has called her several times a day just to tell her he loved her, for which she expressed being "deeply grateful." *Several* times a day. What diligence! This isn't a man who sits around with nothing to do all day and loads of time on his hands. This is an accomplished, hardworking gentleman who also happens to be a devoted husband. How lucky she is. That woman feels the love of her husband, no question.

Many of us can also use our phone to send a quick text message that says "I'm thinking about you," "I just wanted to say I love you," or some other loving note. It doesn't have to say a lot to mean a lot. Sending Scott a text while he is at work is something I've tried to do to help us stay connected. Sometimes I need to remind myself to do it since I'm usually busy with a million little things during the day. But the minute I think of it, I pull out my phone. I type something to him to let him know that I'm thinking of him or that I'm grateful for him. Especially when he was in the thick of launching a new business, and I knew he was dealing with a lot of anxiety, I made this a priority. I often texted him messages that expressed my confidence and belief in him. He later came home on a number of occasions and thanked me, saying "That meant so much to me."

It may seem simple, but this kind of little connection is more fuel for your fire. As Dr. Gottman says, rather than relying on big, flashy vacations, "real-life romance is fueled by a far more humdrum approach to staying connected. It is kept alive each time you let your spouse know he or she is valued during the grind of everyday life. . . . It grows when you know your spouse is having a bad day at work and you take sixty seconds out of your own workday to leave words of encouragement on his voice mail." A simple phone call or text message will do wonders. The ups and downs of using technology in marriage will be explored further in Chapter 6.

Rejoice in Reunions

The way a couple connects after being away has a huge impact on the marriage environment. Researchers have found that the first conversation a couple has after being apart can actually predict marital stability. If the partners seem genuinely interested and excited to see each other, that message connects the couple. On the other hand, consider the wife who shares something that she finds interesting with her husband when he gets home, and he acts uninterested. That reaction can be hurtful. Then, when he tries to share something with her about his workday, she is still irritated from before and can't respond positively. These first greetings have the power to make or break the rest of the evening's interactions.

In his book *Creating an Intimate Marriage*, Dr. Jim Burns shares his simple experiment with a wife who was no longer feeling close to her husband. The woman expressed her frustration that he seemed to drift away from her after coming home from work for the day. Dr. Burns suggested she try something different at his homecoming one evening. Her task was to greet her husband differently. Rather than coming to him with a list of her needs and frustrations, she should try greeting him with a hug and passionate kiss. Then ask him about his day, and refrain from bringing up any trouble spots that evening. Just keep the mood upbeat. Skeptically, she agreed to try.

The next day, she reported to Dr. Burns: "You'll never believe what happened! I did what you suggested, as awkward as it felt to me. He just hung around the kitchen. He helped with dinner. He did the dishes with me. After dinner, instead of going straight to the television, he asked me about my day. We went out later to run an errand together and stopped at a Starbucks just to talk. Jim, you don't understand . . . that was a miracle!" This woman's husband desperately wanted to feel affection from his wife; because she connected positively with him at their reunion, the space between them was full of loving and affectionate energy. He was drawn to her. The rest of the evening was impacted because of her greeting at the door. That's just one evening. Consider the effect of such an environment over time. A simple, loving greeting when a couple reunites can do wonders for a relationship.

Who's Number One?

Any time we show that our spouse is at the top of our list—our "number one"—we communicate love and strengthen our bond. We do that whenever we communicate through word and deed that nothing—not work, not friends, not parents, not hobbies, not TV or the Internet, not even kids—is more important than our spouse.

Several years ago, Scott and I used to meet up for lunch once a week. We lived in San Diego at the time, so I would pick him up at his office downtown then drive ten minutes over to one of my favorite places, Seaport Village. There we would enjoy a picnic lunch and walk around with our son in the stroller. We loved that regular time together. One day after lunch, Scott happened to have a flexible afternoon schedule, and he said, "What if I blow off the rest of the day and we go up to the Wild Animal Park?" I'm sure I had a long list of to-dos, but I was more than happy to drop everything to spend the rest of the day with him. As Scott and I were reminiscing about this time in our life, he shared with me how much it meant to him that I would make these regular lunch dates so important and that I always said "yes" if he had flexibility to play longer. As he explained, "I love that you are so ready to be with me if I have some free time. No matter what it is, if I'm available, you drop everything."

Luckily for me, that's easy to do because I just really like hanging out with Scott. He's a busy guy, so when he has a free moment and he wants to play, I am pretty much always game. It goes both ways. The fact that he wants to be with me whenever he has free time is a reminder of his love. I know I'm his number one. He communicates that even in simple gestures. For example, we love to connect at the end of the day, and when our kids are finally in bed for the night, that's when we usually catch up. Sometimes Scott will be in the middle of some project on his iPad when I come in the room. Usually, he's good about looking up at me and saying, "I'm excited to connect. I just need two minutes to finish something." Right there, he let me know I was his number one, even when he has a whole list of other things on his mind.

Even something as simple as walking our spouse to the door when they are leaving makes an impact. Scott recently told me how much it means to him that I send him off in the morning. "You have a million things you probably want to dive into," he explained, "but this is what you focus on—coming to the door with me. Everything else can wait." That lets him know—in the two minutes it takes me to walk him there, give him a hug, and tell him I'll miss him—that he is more important to me than anything else I could be doing.

Let's be clear—making your spouse your number one does not mean she is the one and only interest in your life. Having personal interests, projects, and friends is important. The point is, your spouse must know and feel that he is at the top of your list by all the things you've done to communicate that. Plus, if your spouse feels he is number one, he will be more inclined to support you in those other interests as well.

Consider how you can let your spouse know she is at the top of your list. If she has a free moment to be with you, let her know you would love nothing more than to join her. At the end of the day, when you finally have a moment together for the first time, give him your undivided attention. Don't just start playing on your phone, reviewing the latest social networking news, or checking your e-mails. (I admit, I have been guilty of this.) Instead, connect with your spouse before you jump into other personal projects. Any time you can, help your spouse feel that if it was a choice between her and any other person, sport, television show, or activity, you would choose her. That simple message makes a difference.

Are You Listening?

We are our spouse's greatest confidant and supporter, which also means that we carry the role of being his or her most important listener. From my perspective, when Scott is willing to listen to what is on my mind, it is healing and connecting. I know he cares about me and what I have to say.

Of course, listening is more than just hearing. As I reminded my daughter recently at dinner, if someone is telling a story and you are pulling on your face and looking the other way, you might be "hearing" the words, but you're not listening. Truly listening involves physical attentiveness through our body language, by showing interest, asking questions to understand, and responding with empathy.

Think about what kind of listener you are. Consider your body language when your spouse is telling you something: Are you facing your spouse? Are you fidgeting? Are you giving your full attention? These simple considerations can help any spouse become a more connected and loving listener. As Scott's Aunt Holly put it, "I feel loved when Chris looks at me, really looks at me, when I speak with him." It's as simple as that.

Next, ask yourself if you make it clear that you are interested in what your spouse has to say. Do you ask questions? Do you nod and give verbal cues that you are listening? Can your spouse tell that you care, even if you aren't *quite* as interested as she is in the topic? I love how my friend Brian described his appreciation of his wife's attempts to show interest in his job as a financial planner. "She dies of boredom every time I begin to talk about my job, but she *acts* like she's interested. Even though I know it's an act, it's also a display that she's showing me she is involved in my life and cares more about me than my actual work." Isn't that great? Sure, this wife isn't all that into financial planning, but she is into her husband. By listening and showing her interest in him, she communicates her love.

Lastly, ask yourself if you are good at conveying your understanding and support after listening to your spouse. It's amazing how great it feels to share with Scott the crazy, frustrating, or funny things that happened during the day and have him just listen and say something as simple as "Wow, that must have been awful having to clean up vomit, spilled milk, and poop in a two-hour period!" Ah, yes, thank you. It was.

As my friend Melinda put it, "One of the things I enjoy most about my marriage and that I think strengthens it on a daily basis is just taking a few minutes to talk and listen to each other. Especially with kids, sometimes I think a few minutes of adult conversation can be priceless. My favorite thing is when my husband takes just a little bit of time to tell me about his day and I can share stories or worries about mine. On the days that we don't get that, I find myself more grouchy and depressed." Indeed, a listening ear is a healing thing.

The trick is determining when to listen and when to problem solve. Sometimes a spouse wants help solving a dilemma, but often, she just wants someone to listen to her thoughts and feelings. (For example: I might not want Scott to tell me that if I just check the lid on the sippy cup a little more thoroughly, then the milk probably wouldn't spill.) If you aren't sure whether your spouse is looking for a brainstorming session, just ask (more on that in Chapter 8). Part of being a good listener is being open to your spouse's thoughts and feelings without passing judgment, and without necessarily looking for a solution. There may be a time to problem solve later, but when a spouse needs to share, the best thing to do is just listen and respond with empathy.

What are the benefits of having a great listener to turn to? Not only does it feel great to have someone who will listen to our hopes, dreams, thoughts, experiences, and concerns, but it is also an important part of managing the stress of daily life. Research shows that a key variable in whether or not couples relapse after marriage therapy is their ability to keep the stress of everyday life from spilling into their relationship. Couples who help each other cope by sharing and listening to each other stay stronger over time.

Whether it's trouble at work, an interesting story on the news, a concern about a child, the desire for a vacation, or a little spilled milk, being a good listener shows that we care what our spouse has to say. The next time your spouse has something to share with you, make it clear that you are ready—and willing—to listen. It isn't difficult to do, but it has a big impact. As my mom's husband, Bob, put it, "Very often, Susie looks into my eyes and smiles when we are talking, even when I am not in the best of moods. That has an amazing healing power and conveys a lot of love."

Be Responsive

In marriage, spouses seek each other's attention and support when they make a comment, ask a question, make a joke, or give a hint. Partners can either respond and turn toward their spouse or they can ignore the bid. Being responsive makes a big impact on the feelings of love and connection in marriage.

The opportunity to respond to your spouse occurs regularly. If I tell Scott that I had the most interesting conversation with my friend today, he has two options: he could either say "Hmm" and keep reading his e-mail (or whatever he happens to be doing) or he could turn toward me and ask, "What did you talk about?"

Scott might say to me, "I had a really frustrating day," and I could either say "I'm sorry" and keep doing whatever I was doing or I could turn toward him and say, "What happened?" Another time, Scott might say, "This new movie came out that looks pretty interesting." I could either say "Oh" and move on or "Oh yeah? Tell me about it."

Do you feel the difference? Turning away or ignoring says "I'm not really interested in what you have to say." On the other hand, responding to and turning toward your spouse says "I want to know about you, what you are interested in, and what you are experiencing." It is a simple thing to do, and yet choosing to respond is a powerful connector.

These are the kinds of interactions Dr. Gottman has dedicated much of his forty-year career to studying. In what he calls his "love lab" (a retreat where couples come to interact for a few days while being observed), Dr. Gottman has found that how a spouse responds to "bids" for attention can have a massive impact on marital happiness. One observation might be that when a husband who loves birds sees a unique finch out the window and points it out to his wife, he is not just telling her something. He is requesting a response. If she responds with, "Oh, that's neat, Honey! Show me!" then she has made a positive response to his bid. If she barely looks up, her marriage may be in trouble. Indeed, in Dr. Gottman's research, the couples who divorced after six years on average only responded positively one-third of the time to each other's bids. On the other hand, couples who were still together after six years responded positively to their spouse's bids nine times out of ten.

Think of what that means! There is a huge relationship between a couple's ability to respond to requests for attention and whether or not they stay together. This does not take a significant amount of time to do. If your spouse wants to tell you something or show you something, then respond! Your marriage depends on it.

As Dr. Gottman also summarizes in his book *10 Lessons to Transform Your Marriage*, "Our research has shown that such exchanges are the stuff that happy marriages are made of. Whether a partner wants sex, affection, conversation, or just some help with the yard work, the story is the same: One partner makes a bid in the form of a comment, a gesture, a question, a touch, or a facial expression. And the other partner 'turns toward' that bid with interest, empathy, or support." Happy couples respond to each other.

The power in this simple action doesn't come from an occasional positive response. This has to be a regular occurrence. As Dr. Gottman explains, "The real secret is to turn toward each other in *little ways* every day. A romantic night out really turns up the heat only when a couple has kept the pilot light burning by staying in touch in the *little ways*." It truly is the small things that we do over time that can make all the difference in our connection. If we get the little things right, like responding to our partner when they seek our attention, then we're on the right path toward a loving, lasting marriage.

I Want What You Want

One of my favorite Dr. Seuss stories is called *The Zax*. In this story, a creature called a Zax is heading north when he runs into another Zax, who is heading south. Neither Zax is willing to move to one side to allow the other Zax to pass. In the end, neither Zax goes anywhere, and an entire city is built around them—complete with a "Zax Overpass." These poor creatures just didn't understand that if they simply took one step to the side, they would both be able to go where they wanted to go.

In marriage, hopefully we're not going in opposite directions, but the principle still stands. The ability to move aside for our spouse is essential in marriage, where we are bound to have different wants and needs from time to time. Marriage research actually shows that spouses who allow themselves to be influenced by their partner have greater ability to influence their partner in return. Spouses who feel that their partner is willing to listen and be persuaded are also less critical in marriage. It just makes sense, right? If I feel that Scott values my opinion and is willing to listen to and be influenced by me, then I feel loved and respected. Knowing he is willing to step my way makes me happy to step his way, too. It is a curious and powerful dance. As a couple, our ability to give strengthens our willingness to sway.

I love watching couples who seem to do this effortlessly, especially those who have been together for decades. They seem to sense what their spouse wants or needs, and rather than complain about their spouse or say "I'm not doing that for you, you big lug," they seem to want to please their spouse however they can. Recently, on a family trip to Yellowstone, we stayed in a little motel run by a husband and wife who had been married for more than thirty years. It was the Fourth of July, and the husband came out to the grill with two steaks on a plate. He turned to us and said, "My wife says she needs steak on the Fourth of July, so I cook steak." Now if that wife was demanding all the time, and if she never did anything for him, this might have been a tough sell. But I got the sense that this was one of those couples who found pleasure in fulfilling each other's desires. The same thing can be said for my neighbors Bob and Carol. When I asked if he liked doing what she asked him to do, he said, "Yes. And I've learned the sooner, the better!"

Laws of Attraction

I think most people would agree that what's on the outside is not the most important part of a fulfilling marriage relationship. But think back for a moment to when you were dating your spouse. Wasn't it fun to find him at the door with nicely combed hair, a fresh shave, and a splash of cologne? Didn't you love seeing her waiting for you at the restaurant, looking lovely, knowing she dressed up for *you?* Wasn't that physical attraction at least part of why you fell in love in the first place? Even now, doesn't it feel exciting to see that your spouse still wants to impress you?

I remember sitting in a media theory class in graduate school. The fairly feminist professor pulled out a women's magazine from the 1950s. She opened the page to an article about what to do when your hubby comes home. In the article, the writer encouraged wives to freshen up and put on a little lipstick before their man walked through the door. We all scoffed. I even found myself thinking, *Pulleeeease. That is ridiculous. I don't need to impress my man. He loves me just the way I am.*

Of course he does. But do I still want to impress him? *Should* I? Let's think about this. Yes, Scott should love me just the way I am, and if I want (or need) to have an I-didn't-make-it-to-the-shower kind of day, he shouldn't think any less of me. Indeed, I get more compliments from my honey when I'm sporting jeans, a T-shirt, and a ponytail than at any other time—though I still haven't figured that one out. The point is, if we go out of our way to look great for our spouse, then that is rewarding for everyone. It's fun to look nice and feel good. (To achieve that goal, we might consider regular exercise, good hygiene, a healthy diet, and clothes that fit right.) It's also fun for the spouse who gets to enjoy their partner looking great.

It might be easy to feel intimidated by that suggestion, but remember that when you married your spouse, surely physical attraction played a role. The important thing to note is that attraction is still important, no matter the effects of time over the years. I find my husband even more handsome now—with the smile lines around his eyes and flecks of grey in his hair—than ever before. We can all make an effort to look our best, for our spouse but also for ourselves. It feels good to look good.

From a two-minute perspective, all it takes is combing your hair nicely, choosing an outfit that looks good and fits well, getting that breath minty fresh for date night, and, yes, even a little lip gloss or cologne will do. If you're feeling brave, let your spouse have a free pass to remove any undesirable items from your closet. I once heard a story on a radio program about a woman who did this. When she and her husband were just dating, she used to wear her favorite tight, leopard-skin pants. She thought she looked darn good in those pants, so she often wore them on dates with him. After they were married, she let her husband raid her closet to get rid of anything he detested. What was the first article he pulled out of her closet? The leopard-skin pants! It's a good testament to the fact that it really is what's on the inside that counts most (he fell in love despite the pants).

So, yes, what's on the inside counts most, but the outside matters, too. The next time you go out, prepare with your spouse in mind. Even on a daily basis, consider ways to make your spouse smile with your appearance. When Scott changes after work, he sprays on a little cologne just for me. That has a surprising impact. I try to shower and look nice, even if the only other adult I am seeing all day long is Scott. (He's the most important one anyway.) The point is, we are still showing each other we care to impress. It may not be the most important thing in marriage, but feeling that tingle of physical attraction is a fun and important part of a lifelong courtship.

Be Playful

Have you ever heard this statement: "The couple who plays together stays together"? According to Howard Markman, a psychologist who co-directs the University of Denver's Center for Marital and Family Studies, that's pretty much true. In an interview with *USA Today*, Markman explained, "The more you invest in fun and friendship and being there for your partner, the happier the relationship will get over time. The correlation between fun and marital happiness is high, and significant."

Playing together builds connections and strengthens relationships. For example, take the husband who for years would hide objects under the covers on his wife's side of the bed to scare her and then laugh with her. With a silly gesture, he's communicating that making her smile is important to him. In another example, because Scott once teased me about the minuscule amount of toothpaste I put on his toothbrush, the next night I put so much on that it was glopping down the side of his toothbrush and onto the sink. He laughed and returned the favor the next night. We were just being silly together, connecting through play.

Something else that we do—just for fun—is pass a little flyer that we got years ago at a business dinner back and forth between us. It has a picture of a former governor of Utah on it. I can't remember how the object became significant to us, but somehow we started hiding it in each other's things. When one of us finds it, we promptly find a new hiding place. Months will go by, and I will open a folder or book and be surprised to find "The Governor," as we've dubbed it. I'll chuckle and then hide it in one of Scott's books or briefcases for him to find later. Today, I honestly don't know where The Governor is, but I know he'll turn up again at some point. (I must note that, after I initially wrote this section, I found The Governor in a book I started reading last year but hadn't picked up for months. Now, The Governor is hiding in Scott's briefcase.)

Even a little tickle or pat can add playfulness to your relationship. Take Carol and Bob, for example. When I asked Carol how she felt loved, one of the things she mentioned was that whenever she walks by, Bob will pat her on the backside. I asked if she liked that, and she giggled and said, "Yeah, I know it's just a love pat." Apparently he has to be careful when they're in a public place with lots of other backsides. "I have to make sure I've got the right woman!" he laughed. In return, she often tickles him. I asked Bob if he liked that. He said, "No!" but he chuckled and looked at her when he said it. I'm guessing he would miss it if she were to stop one day. The playful attention says, "I'm interested in you."

Find ways to be playful in your marriage. Having inside jokes or just doing things that make each other smile is a powerful and fun way to connect.

Be Attentive

Being attentive to your spouse's needs is another way to build loving connections. If your husband is outside sweating in the yard, he would probably love a drink of water. Even better, he would probably love a drink of water from *his wife*. If your spouse just had a long day on her feet, she could probably use a foot rub, and she would especially love a foot rub from *her husband*. Multiple times a day, if you are watching, you can find opportunities to attend to your spouse and show your love.

When I asked Scott how he felt loved in our marriage, he said how important my being in tune with his needs is to him. He said, "Sometimes I'll come home and be obviously tired and worn out. You'll just say 'Go ahead upstairs and check out.' That you're even offering that when I know you're probably tired too means a lot on a whole lot of levels. It says (1) you're paying attention and are in tune with what I'm experiencing, and (2) you care enough to offer a solution that involves a sacrifice."

Pay attention to how your spouse is feeling. My friend Diana has been happily married for forty-eight years and she says, "Even in church, when the air conditioner is running and I am feeling cold, he will remove his suit coat and put it around my shoulders. He is always concerned about my comfort and safety." She feels her husband's love through his simple gestures of courtesy.

Being aware of your spouse's needs and doing what you can to provide comfort is a simple way to show love. I know, in my marriage, I love being the one to bring my husband comfort. As Scott has expressed to me on a number of occasions, "You are my refuge." That is what I always want to be for him.

Walk Down Memory Lane

Part of building the connections that pull you together is reminiscing about the enjoyable times in your past. Marriage research shows that remembering positive times in your marriage strengthens your bond. Indeed, according to Dr. Gottman, 94 percent of the time, when couples take time to look back on their history together with fondness, they are likely to have a happy future together.

The other night, Scott and I were out to dinner and were reminiscing about some of our silly and memorable moments. We recalled the time when we went to the state fair and Scott agreed to accompany me on my favorite ride, the Zipper, which involves little cages that flip in complete circles as they move around a rotating outer belt. He detests the ride, but he wanted to do it for me. (We agreed that it should be recorded somewhere that his phone fell out of his pocket on that ride when we were flung upside down, and he thought it was gone for good. Then it miraculously came floating up in front of his face during a flip and he caught it midair. But I digress.) Scott was so shaken from that ride that he didn't speak for a good half hour afterward. Still, he had made his loving sacrifice. The recollection made us both smile.

We also talked that night at dinner about how I always notice when the time is 8:18, because our wedding anniversary is August 18. I never knew, but Scott recently told me he loves that I do that, because it shows how much I value that date. Our kids even smile when I say, "It's 8:18!" We continued enjoying pieces of our history that night, connecting through the experiences in our past. Swimming in the past for a bit helps us feel the loving feelings we've enjoyed before and allows us to realize, in the present, the depth and joy of our relationship.

It can be helpful to remember the good times, even when you're in the middle of a hard time—and, let's face it, all marriages go through hard times. As one husband put it, "Looking back with fondness on happy moments together helps me remember that it wasn't always this hard." Remembering your happy times in the past renews loving feelings in the present and brings hope for a happy future.

Take moments to remember your favorite times together. Look at your wedding album together and remember how you felt that day. Revisit the days when you bought your first home or when a child was born. Recall happy moments when you dated or vacationed or had a romantic evening. Remember silly things you did for each other. Re-live it. Remembering pulls you back to that moment in time, bringing back all the wonderful feelings you had then. As Alan Jackson sings in one of my favorite country songs, "Remember when the sound of little feet was the music we danced to week to week. Brought back the love, we found trust. Vowed we'd never give it up. Remember when."

Love through Music

You and your spouse probably have a song that is *your* song. In two or three minutes, that special song can evoke powerful memories and deeply loving feelings. This isn't strategic! You aren't tricking your spouse into feeling love for you. You are simply doing what you probably did a lot when you were first dating and falling in love. Remember your falling-in-love feelings and what role music played in your courtship. Playing that special song for your spouse is a simple way to tell your spouse, "I'm *still* thinking of you." No doubt, the song will probably mean more now than it did then.

I had the opportunity to experience this powerful connecting force recently in a car ride with Scott and our kids. Scott was in the driver's seat, letting everyone take a turn choosing his or her favorite song. When it was Scott's turn, he didn't say anything for a moment while he scrolled down his playlist. Suddenly, the words from our song, "Everything I Do" by Bryan Adams, came pouring out of the speakers. I sat and listened as the words about what one person can mean to another flowed through the speakers. Talk about tingles. This became our song when we were first falling in love. We danced to it at our wedding. Now here we were, sitting in our car, with sixteen years of marriage and four little ones behind us. Those words reached me, more true and powerful than they ever had before.

My father-in-law expressed to me how much music means to him in marriage. He is a musician and has a great appreciation for the emotion that comes with music. On his wife's fiftieth birthday, they went to San Francisco to celebrate. After dinner, they danced at a restaurant called Top of the Mark, with a gorgeous view of the city. Now, whenever he hears one of the songs they danced to that night, he remembers their happy time together.

Singing a song to your spouse is another way to connect through music. My friend Diana told me that her husband will often sing to her over and over while he's in the shower, "Oh, Diana, I love you . . ." As she said, "That means a lot to me." If you have the voice or the inclination, feel free to belt out a love song.

Another option is to write out the lyrics of a love song you like. My friend Stacey likes to instant message lyrics with her husband when they are apart. She said, "During busy season, Jake and I never see each other. After I get the kids down for the night, I usually try to get some work done. There have been a couple times when he is working late at the office and I am working late at home, and we IM. Either he or I will be listening to some love song and will send the lyrics over IM. Then we will both listen to the song and send each other phrases. It may sound cheesy, but it is actually very romantic."

Whether it's playing your special song, remembering a romantic moment together through music, singing a love song, or instant messaging lyrics when you're apart, loving your spouse through music is a simple and powerful way to connect.

Ask Your Spouse out

Almost nothing says "I love you" more than the offer to spend time together. By asking your spouse out on a date, you are saying, "I like the person you are, and I want to be with you."

The other day, I was talking to a good friend of mine who has had a bit of a bumpy road in marriage. One Tuesday morning, his wife came to him and let him know that she was planning to go on a big hike the next morning. Then she asked, "Would you like to go with me?" With that simple question, he felt loved. "I really liked that she asked," he said.

I love it when Scott asks me out. Going out on a date night once a week is pretty routine for us. It's a time when we both look forward to getting away, just the two of us, to talk, play, and connect. Usually we'll just assume it's a go, and we'll talk about what we want to do. But then there are times when weekends get busy, and we'll go a few weeks without getting in that precious time. Recently, we went through a stretch like that, and Scott came to me and said, "Will you go on a date with me this weekend?" I had to smile. I was just tickled that he would ask me out like that, as though we were teenagers. He even brainstormed some ideas with me and called a sitter. The date itself, obviously, is a bigger opportunity to connect. Yet merely in making the offer, Scott made a connection with me. In that moment, we drew closer than we were before.

Letting your spouse know you want that time together is key. Scott recently told me how much that prioritizing means to him. "You're juggling so much," he said. "That effort to schedule our date means so much. The kids sometimes will stay up later, and sometimes the house is a mess when we get home. There's an impact. But you do it because it's important to you. It shows our relationship doesn't take second place to hobbies or errands. You make us most important." That's true. That time together is important to me. The bonding and connecting that takes place on the actual date is wonderful. But simply by communicating to each other that we want a date and are going to make it happen shows how much we love each other.

Find a time to ask your spouse out. Call him up at work, write her a note, or ask for a date over dinner at home. Let your spouse know you would love nothing more than to spend an evening together. Make a plan. Your spouse will love knowing you care about your time together.

Loving Touch

Scientists have long known what a big impact physical affection has on newborn babies. Human beings simply need to connect physically with other human beings in order to thrive. Being physically affectionate with each other is an important way for a couple to connect, literally. Something as simple as a lingering hug even releases hormones that relax and heal. Psychology professor Sonja Lyubomirsky writes, "A pat on the back, a squeeze of the hand, a hug, an arm around the shoulder—the science of touch suggests that it can save a so-so marriage. Introducing more (nonsexual) touching and affection on a daily basis will go a long way in rekindling the warmth and tenderness."

My mom is a labor and delivery nurse who has long shifts at the hospital. She often comes home aching from head to toe. When I asked her how she feels loved by her husband, the first thing she thought of was how much she loves when Bob takes care of her physically by massaging her feet or back. Even when she was studying for a big nursing exam, he attended to her. "Every time he came into the room where I was studying," she said, "he would stop to massage my neck and shoulders for a couple of minutes. That was so sweet."

Hugs can be a powerful and thoughtful connector as well. Researchers at Penn State University found that students who were asked to give or receive at least five hugs a day over the course of a month were significantly happier than the non-hugging students in the study. So, hug away! You will feel more connected to your spouse and happier, too.

There are so many ways to show love through physical affection. When I asked one husband how he felt loved by his wife, the first thing he said was, "The other day, my wife just came up to me out of the blue and gave me a kiss. Not for a greeting or anything that's routine, but just because she knew I'd appreciate it. That really let me know she was thinking about me." My neighbor Carol, speaking of her husband, said, "I love it when he comes up behind me and kisses me on the neck." One of my good friends told me how much he loves when his wife plays with his hair. Another friend expressed to me how much she loves when her husband will scratch her back or arm for a few minutes when they are going to bed. She knows, in those moments, that he wants her to be comfortable.

I've been surprised to realize how much it means to me when Scott passes by me somewhere in the house and stops to just put his hand on my back or my shoulder. Even while I was sitting down writing this chapter, Scott came down the stairs, leaned over, and kissed me on top of the head on his way to the kitchen. That made me smile. Whatever it is—hugging, kissing, giving a foot rub, playing with each other's hair, or holding hands when you walk down the street—making an effort to connect physically is one more simple way to tell your spouse, "I love you."

Connect Spiritually

When Scott and I have the opportunity to discuss some of the more meaningful things in life—like why we are here, what we are grateful for, things we are learning, and areas in which we are struggling—I'm always amazed at how connected I feel to him. Although there are many ways to have these deeply connecting moments, one of our favorite ways to reflect is in prayer, something that three-quarters of Americans report doing regularly. We enjoy this opportunity to open ourselves up to a higher power, to humbly express our gratitude, and to ask for help with concerns. It also allows us to be more in tune with each other. As Scott put it, "I like hearing you pray. It's a reminder of what's on your mind and an opportunity to be reminded of our common goals and blessings. There's also something powerful about kneeling, holding hands, and feeling unified in our life together."

Researchers at Brigham Young University and Florida State University have discovered many the benefits of marital prayer (which surely applies similarly to couples' meditation or thoughtful reflection). Couples who pray together feel better able to prioritize their relationship over individual needs, they gain clarity in regard to their relationship concerns, their angry feelings are softened, they are more willing to forgive, they trust each other more, and their health is even improved through relaxation and increased brain activity. You don't have to be religious to gain the benefits that come from this kind of unified reflection. The point is, couples will find power in the opportunity to open up to each other on a regular basis about their thoughts, feelings, blessings, struggles, and concerns.

Take time to dig deeper in your relationship and feel the benefits. Pray together, if that works for you, or find a way to reflect on your life together. Feel the humility that comes from being on your knees and seeking answers outside yourselves. Talk about the things you are grateful for in your life together. Be open about your concerns. Share insights you've gained from your daily experiences. Or simply step outside together and enjoy the beauties of nature. As Scott's dad said, "Just going out together and sharing a starry night, taking in the wonders of the world, helps me feel connected to my spouse." Find ways to connect spiritually with your spouse, and feel the unifying force those moments can bring.

Every day brings opportunities to love our spouse in a thousand different ways. It doesn't have to be a love sonnet off the balcony (although if you feel so inclined, go for it!). Ask yourself the question from one of my favorite songs in the movie *Enchanted*, "How does she know you love her?" How does he know you love him? You have to *do* something! What have you done to show your love lately? Bring home a surprise, call to say he's been on your mind, send her a text message, polish his shoes, leave a love note in her purse, reminisce about your favorite times together, give him a foot rub, bring her some orange juice, play the song that means so much to you both, or say a prayer together. Do it without expecting anything in return. It doesn't take long to show that you care. These are not just the actions of couples falling in love. These are the actions of couples who want to *stay* in love for the long haul.

TWO-MINUTE ACTION STEPS

(COMPLETE ONCE AND REPEAT OFTEN):

Think about your rituals as a couple. If you can't think of any, create one. Find something that is meaningful only to the two of you—silly or serious—and practice it regularly to connect.

Find a way to serve your spouse, without being asked, simply because you want to communicate your love.

Invite your spouse to take some personal time to do what he or she loves.

Leave a love note somewhere that will surprise your spouse, such as on the steering wheel, on the mirror, or in the fridge.

Call or text your spouse to share your love and gratitude.

The next time you come together after you've been apart, give your spouse a great greeting.

Think about the things that are important in your life. Ask yourself, *Is my spouse at the top of my list?* The next time you have to choose between giving your attention to your spouse or something else—kids, neighbors, a social media site, or a football game—let your spouse know he or she is number one.

The next time your spouse is telling you something, show you are listening with your body language and attention. Let your spouse know you care what he or she has to say.

The next time your spouse makes a bid for your attention, respond. Be available and supportive through your gestures, your questions, and your input.

The next time your spouse asks something of you, if you can, be willing to say "Yes."

Consider how you prepared for a date with your spouse before you were married, then on your next date, dress to impress.

Do something to make your spouse smile.

Watch for opportunities to attend to your spouse's needs, such as bringing a drink of water on a hot day or offering a jacket when it's cold.

Bring up a cherished memory from your shared history and reminisce with your spouse.

Play or sing "your song" for your spouse at home or in the car.

Ask your spouse out on a date and make a few creative suggestions for what you could do together.

Surprise your spouse with a kiss or tender embrace when it's not expected.

Find a way to connect spiritually with your spouse, whether through prayer, couples' meditation, thoughtful reflection, or quiet time in nature. Feel the connecting force those moments can bring.

Chapter 6

Going Digital: The Good, the Bad, and the Ugly

Even the technology that promises to unite us, divides us. Each of us is now electronically connected to the globe, and yet we feel utterly alone.

— **Dan Brown,** *Angels & Demons*

There is no getting around it—we live in a technological age. Everywhere we look, we see some kind of screen: on the wall, on the dresser, on the desk, on the table, at our work, in our homes, or in our hands. Many incredible advances and opportunities come with this age. More information is at our fingertips than ever before. Connecting with our loved ones—even when they are on the other side of the world—has never been easier. We can capture our own experiences and share them in seconds with the people who matter most to us. At the same time, we have to be careful. Being more "connected" than ever has its drawbacks. Suddenly, as we fiddle with our phones and surf the waves of social media, we can sometimes become more disconnected to the people we love the most—maybe even the person sitting right next to us. Thus, with great technology comes great responsibility. This chapter will explore how technology can impact your marriage, for better and for worse.

The Good

My husband, Scott, works a lot. Not as much as he used to as a lawyer, but still, he leaves the house most days before 8 a.m. and doesn't get home until just before 7:00. Then, because of church responsibilities, he is away two or three evenings a week and most of the day on Sunday serving our neighborhood. He is engaged in wonderful things, and I am happy to support him. What makes it easier is our ability to connect through technology, even though we are apart.

We generally try to talk for a few minutes at some point during the day simply to share how the day is going. Indeed, while I was sitting here writing this chapter, I received a phone call from Scott, who was driving back from a client lunch and wanted to tell me about how much he is enjoying a newfound friendship. During our conversations, I might share with him something I did with the kids, or about a writing project I'm working on, or a funny thing that happened while I was volunteering at the school. Sometimes we send pictures to each other that capture something interesting or beautiful we saw. Or, I might text him to say, "Hey honey, I hope you are having a great day. Thanks for all you do." I know it doesn't sound like much, but he says that means a lot to him. That little gesture shows that I am thinking about him. I know I feel the same when he sends me a little digital love note.

It doesn't take long to make the connection. Use technology to connect with your spouse during the day and to share your love. Whether through a phone call, an e-mail, a text, a photo, a voice message, or a video chat when you are apart, take the opportunity to love your spouse digitally. Just be careful to keep it simple. One study by the Oxford Internet Institute surveyed 3,500 couples and found that couples who used more than five channels of communication (including Facebook, e-mails, texts, tweets and instant messages) to connect with their spouse actually had a drop of 14 percent in marital satisfaction. The researchers performing the study suggest that may have something to do with the pressure of maintaining so many communication channels at once. So keeping it to your top two or three favorite methods might do the trick. For me, receiving a phone call or text message from my honey is a sure way to brighten my day (assuming it's a sweet message of love, affection, humor, or gratitude. Reminders or requests to take out the trash or pick up the dry cleaning don't count!).

Watching a television show or playing video games together can also boost the loving feelings in your relationship, provided you are both excited about the prospect. Researchers at Brigham Young University recently surveyed married couples and found that when both people were excited about playing, 76 percent said that gaming has a positive effect on their marital relationship. The number of hours of playtime didn't necessarily make a difference. The important factor to consider is "whether or not it creates conflict and quarreling over the game," said Recreation Management Professor Neil Lundberg. For Scott and me, watching an episode of *Frasier* or at the end of the day is a fun way for us to relax and laugh together. Do what works for you.

There are plenty of ways to use your digital savvy to bless your relationship. If you find a way to use technology to make your spouse smile, to feel closer, or to simply help your spouse know that he or she is on your mind, then go for it. The trouble comes when you use that same technology to connect with the many other people who are available and waiting for your attention.

The Bad

Using technology to connect with our spouse in positive ways can strengthen marriage. However, connecting with our Facebook friends or posting pictures on Instagram needs moderation if we're going to keep our number one feeling like number one. This modern-era addiction is becoming increasingly difficult to drop. In fact, according to a recent study reported by the *New York Times*, women now spend twelve hours more per week on their smartphones than with their partner! Sure, social media sites are a fun way to share and connect. The trick is to make sure we aren't doing it so much that we are sacrificing time with our most important person. As marriage therapist Dr. Kent Griffiths put it, "Young couples, in particular, have so little time with one another with the demands of children, career, and maintaining home and lifestyle. To spend scarce free time on social media removes precious opportunity when they could otherwise be connecting. Social media is our way of joining with the world, but needs to be managed in terms of its time and importance."

Especially at night, screens are simply bad company. Dr. Alicia Clark, a Washington DC psychologist, reported to the *Huffington Post* that being on a screen at night surfing social media can be damaging to your relationship for many reasons. "Not only are you on your computer screen when your partner might be interested in relationship-enhancing conversation, physical intimacy, or a cuddle, you are likely tinkering with your natural sleep cues that could leave you sleep deprived," she said. "As I've told clients, avoid social media (and screens) at least one hour before bed in order to help you get the best sleep possible and so you can engage with your partner instead. Keep the bedroom a screen-free zone."

Don't let your gadgets interfere with your ability to have a happy and fulfilling partnership with the person right there next to you. Here are a few questions to ask yourself: Am I spending more time posting on social media than I am spending with my spouse? Am I on my phone or computer at night or in bed when I otherwise might be able to engage meaningfully with my partner? Has my partner expressed frustration with the amount of time I spend on social media sites? Am I more concerned about what is happening on Facebook than about what my spouse is doing right next to me? If the answer to any of these questions is "yes," then it's time to make a change.

The Ugly

Connecting through technology can move beyond being a simple distraction and become a serious threat to the happiness of your marriage. This is the dark side of technology, home to two of the worst culprits of emotional infidelity: social media sites and pornography.

As of January 2014, 74 percent of adults had a Facebook account. According to Amanda Lenhart, a senior researcher with Pew Internet and American Life Project at Pew Research Center, while 89 percent of adults said they used their online profiles to "stay in touch with friends," 20 percent said they used it "to flirt." If you think that seems innocent enough, consider that one-third of divorce cases cited social media as part of the problem.

Flirting of any kind, either with an old flame or a new friend, can be potentially harmful to your marriage. What starts innocently enough can all too easily become something it was never meant to be. According to Psychologist John Grohol, the CEO and founder of Psych Central, "Readily available communication on Facebook leads people to pursue temptation or engage in risky behaviors.

Facebook makes it easy to engage in less inhibited communication—which can lead to taking risks we wouldn't ordinarily take in our everyday life."

Dr. Grohol shares the story of one of his clients, Amy, who had been happily married for more than eight years when she accepted a friend request from an old love, thinking it would be fun and harmless to catch up. "Amy started messaging him through Facebook, and the more they talked, the more they also began to flirt," Dr. Grohol said. "Flirting made her feel special and a little reckless, two things that were missing from her predictable marriage. It started off harmless enough, but over time, it started to get more and more serious. Finally, Amy decided to meet up with Joe for a drink. That bad decision led to another—to sleep with him."

The same sort of situation was underway with another couple, marriage educators K. Jason and Kelli Krafsky, authors of *The Social Media Couple*. When Kelli started catching up via Facebook with her first love, she was having a rush of happy memories and emotions, while her husband started feeling pangs of anxiety and jealousy. The couple started talking about what was happening and reversed course before any more damage was done. "We came to the conclusion that having Facebook friendships with exes wasn't good for our marriage," says Jason.

Keep in mind that you can be emotionally unfaithful to your spouse just as much as you can be physically unfaithful. Even becoming emotionally involved with someone of the opposite sex puts a hurtful wedge between you and your spouse. Talk to your spouse about what you are both comfortable with in terms of connecting with members of the opposite sex and consider ruling out connecting with old flames.

Beyond giving the ability to connect inappropriately on social media, the Internet also provides access to the other ugly technological weapon that is destroying marriages by the minute:

pornography. Both men and women can be hurt drastically by the effects of pornography. One 2004 study found that its use is so rampant that 56 percent of divorce cases involved one party being obsessed with pornographic websites. In another study in 2003, the American Academy of Matrimonial Lawyers polled 350 divorce attorneys and found that two-thirds of them reported that the Internet played a significant role in the divorces, with interest in online pornography contributing to more than half of the cases.

According to clinical therapist Dr. Peter Kleponis, PA, the use of pornography is a violation of marital trust to love and honor each other. He explains, "Viewing pornography is akin to breaking these vows because they are in no way a sign of a man's love, honor, and respect for his wife. For these women, the men they married all of a sudden seem like strangers. Many feel like a fool for ever having trusted their husbands. For some women, the violation of trust is so deep that they question if they can go on with their marriage. . . . Pornography invading the home can also lead a wife to feel old, unattractive, and sexually undesirable."

Besides these negative effects, even brief repeated exposure to pornography can impact a man's ability to be intimate with his wife because "what was once sexually arousing becomes boring and uninteresting," according to Dr. Kleponis. More importantly, it robs a man of the ability to be respected by his wife, which studies show for most men is even more important than their need to be loved (indeed, in a study of 400 men, 74 percent said they would rather feel alone and unloved than disrespected and inadequate).

To avoid the kind of serious damage that can come along with pornography, the simplest, safest plan of action is to avoid it altogether. Consider using Internet filtering methods to limit the kinds of images that can come into your home and keep an open dialogue with each other about how you will safeguard your marriage.

What to Do

Absolutely use technology in your marriage! Use it to connect when you are apart, to share moments from your day, and even to enjoy a good show or video game together. In other words, use technology to enrich and strengthen your relationship.

But be aware of how you are using technology, and consider whether you are distracted by it. Are you spending more time connecting with others through your gadgets than with the person sitting right next to you? Remind yourself how important this person is to you, and be sure to invest in that relationship first and foremost.

For the health of your marriage, avoid using technology in any way that will damage the trust between you or cause feelings of jealousy, irritation, lack of respect, or unfaithfulness. Have an open discussion about who you will connect with online and agree on reasonable amounts of screen time. Above all, remember that the person you love is right there waiting for—and needing—your attention. Don't let the little screen take anything away from you.

Two-Minute Action Steps

(COMPLETE ONCE AND REPEAT OFTEN):

Think about how you use technology in positive ways to connect with your spouse. How do you regularly reach out with phone calls, e-mails, and texts when you are apart? The next time your spouse has been away for more than an hour, send a photo or a message that communicates your love.

Think about how much you use technology in the evening when your spouse is home. Are you spending more time on your phone than you are interacting with your partner? Tonight, make a goal to have your bedroom be technology-free.

Consider whether you have ever used a social media site to flirt with an old flame or used the Internet to view something that would make your spouse uncomfortable. Make a date to talk to your spouse about rules for using the Internet and commit doing only what will benefit your marriage.

Chapter 7

Get a Little Closer: Small Steps toward Great Intimacy

Love is of all passions the strongest, for it attacks simultaneously the head, the heart, and the senses.

—**Lao Tzu,** Chinese spiritual leader

Maybe it's risky to have a chapter on physical intimacy in a marriage book about two-minute tips. The very juxtaposition of these topics makes me think of a funny YouTube musical spoof by Flight of the Conchords. In this song about "business time" in marriage, the singer suggests that his wife shouldn't be disappointed because "two minutes in heaven is better than one minute in heaven." Scott and I laugh every time we quote that phrase. It's ridiculous, and yet, sadly, there is some truth to this minor detail: men and women sometimes just don't get each other when it comes to being intimate. There are, however, a few key ingredients that can make a big difference, even in an area as important and powerful as a couple's love life.

First Key Ingredient: Emotional Intimacy

The first, and most important, thing for every couple to understand is that emotional intimacy paves the way for enjoyable physical intimacy. Emotional intimacy is the atmosphere in marriage, whereas physical intimacy is an event. That is not to trivialize the event, which has the potential to bring great passion, enjoyment, and closeness for two partners. Nonetheless, the event can only be great if the emotional environment is great.

According to marriage researcher Dr. John Gottman, "the determining factor in whether couples feel satisfied with the sex, romance, and passion in their marriages is, by 70 percent, the quality of the couples' friendship." In other words, a couple's feelings of friendship and bonding are critically important. It is that intimate bonding that occurs when two people share their hopes, their dreams, their fears, and their time. It involves talking together, working together, playing together, and building a life together. It is what happens when each person feels listened to, cared for, respected, understood, and loved.

So ask yourself: how is your friendship? Everything in this book so far has been geared toward doing the small and simple things that can make a huge difference for the feelings of intimate connection in marriage. Those things, which are greatly rewarding in and of themselves, can also create the emotional bond that can then set the stage for an enjoyable love life. Consistently sharing loving words and deeds builds the healthy emotional environment that is so critical in marriage.

A strong friendship also allows each person to fully give himself or herself. As counselor G. Hugh Allred has noted, "Both [spouses] must work to be respectful, courteous and loving with each other in all areas of their interaction so they can give freely and without fear of being hurt in this most intimate of relationships." When a person feels respected, admired, needed, trusted, secure, and loved in every other area of marriage, being physically intimate can be exactly what it is supposed to be: a powerful time for two people to connect in a way that they don't with anyone else.

Second Key Ingredient: Appreciate the Importance

Being physically intimate with each other is a normal, healthy, and important part of marriage. It is a way for a couple to share affection, tenderness, and passion in a connection like no other. Not only is lovemaking a powerful bonding experience, but it is also actually good for your health. According to a report in *Women's Health Magazine*, people who make love regularly are better able to relax and manage their stress. Dr. Laura Berman, a clinical professor of obstetrics-gynecology and psychiatry, says the experience is so powerful because endorphins and oxytocin are released during lovemaking, and these feel-good hormones activate pleasure centers in the brain that bolster feelings of intimacy and relaxation. The science goes to show that the effects of the moment are more than momentary.

Physical intimacy is important enough to be somewhere on your marital agenda. If life is busy and you find yourselves out of energy and desire at the end of the day, consider including an intimate night on your weekly roster. As terribly unromantic as it sounds, if partners wait until both feel swept away in the moment, they may be waiting for months. Physical intimacy is so vital for the romance and connection in marriage that most experts agree it's best for your relationship if you engage at least once a week. Consider marking your calendar.

Here's one couple who does just that. In his book *Creating an Intimate Marriage*, Dr. Jim Burns shares his friend's sassy secret. Every Wednesday night is this couple's romantic night. Both the husband and wife look forward to it. In the morning, they look at each other and say, "It's Wednesday!" The wife sometimes e-mails her husband during the day to say "It's Wednesday!" Is this a boring routine? Humdrum and unromantic? For this couple, having a planned event is fun and exciting. Sometimes it's just making the effort to get in the mood. Think back to your wedding day. Was the expectation of your wedding night boring and un-spontaneous? Or were you filled with excited anticipation as you looked forward to an evening of intimacy?

However you choose to make it happen, find a way to make your love life an important and regular part of your marriage relationship. Do it for your couple connection, for the fun of it, and for your health.

Third Key Ingredient: Understand Differences

For a healthy love life, husband and wife must both appreciate the importance of this bonding experience while also understanding each other's unique needs. Research by internationally renowned marriage expert and author Dr. Willard Harley says the drive for physical intimacy comes more easily to men, while women are more naturally affectionate. I once heard it put this way: men are like microwaves and women are like slow cookers. Men heat up and cool down quickly (hence the two minutes in heaven joke).

Women need more time. We're just wired differently. Understanding and acknowledging those differences can lead to a great love life for both partners. In his book *His Needs, Her Needs*, Dr. Harley explains why:

> While probably more in touch with their own sexuality because it is such a basic male drive, many men lack skill in lovemaking because they fail to understand a woman's need for affection as part of the sexual process. When a man learns to be affectionate, his lovemaking will become very different. . . . Conversely, many women don't understand their own sexuality well enough to know how to enjoy meeting a husband's compelling need for sex. To satisfy her husband sexually, a wife must also feel satisfied. I try to encourage wives . . . to commit themselves to learning to enjoy the sex relationship as much as their husband does.

Some couples have less experience in this world than others when they wed. Many have no experience at all and even feel that talking about it is taboo. Sure, you can learn through trial and error and lots of open communication. Alternatively, consider picking up a tasteful book that discusses the differences in male and female chemistry and anatomy. Surely a helpful librarian or bookstore employee can point you in the right direction. Don't be shy! Remember, this is an experience that you can enjoy regularly your whole marriage—be sure you understand how to make it great for both of you.

Fourth Key Ingredient: Set the Stage

Creating a romantic atmosphere can help a person unwind, relax, and feel open to an intimate experience. Candles, lingerie, music, a bubble bath, and massage oil are fun and simple things that can have a powerful impact on mood. In addition, don't underestimate the power of language in setting the stage. We all want to know our partner finds us attractive. Share with each other what you find handsome, beautiful, or sexy. However it works for you, create your romantic oasis, a refuge from the storms of the outside world where you can melt into the moment.

Your oasis doesn't have to be a same-place, same-time kind of experience. I recently read an article about an intriguing concept called *sacanagem*, which is a Portuguese word that basically means, "Let's experiment." The idea of sacanagem is to have fun and try new things in bed—or even elsewhere. Be adventurous. Think about how you can mix things up in your relationship, and add some variety to your routine. Psychology professor Sonja Lyubomirsky says that mixing things up is important because, as human beings, we get used to doing the same things over and over, and then we stop enjoying them as much. Part of keeping love alive is exploring new ways to experience it.

Essential in the lead up to any experience is a tender, affectionate warm-up. A loving embrace and passionate kiss may be more intimate than anything else you could do to keep the romantic fires burning. According to marriage therapist Dr. Jim Burns, "Couples who don't kiss passionately often feel sexually and emotionally abandoned. Kissing is personal, and it is often a good indication of the quality of your marriage relationship." Dr. Burns's research also shows that couples who take time to hug, lie next to each other, and simply touch each other create a powerful, emotional bonding experience.

It doesn't take long—light a candle, fill the bath, turn on a song, touch tenderly. These are simple ways to set the stage for a romantic experience.

Fifth Key Ingredient: Communicate

What is your spouse's favorite way to warm up? Favorite place to be touched? Favorite way to be kissed? If you don't know, then find out! Explore your own likes and dislikes, and let your spouse know about them. Don't assume your spouse already knows (or should know) everything about you. Certainly don't assume your spouse likes everything just the way you do. Communicating openly is an important step for both partners in creating a mutually enjoyable experience. Don't be hesitant to share your thoughts. Even if what you want seems silly, share your ideas. You might be surprised at how willing your spouse is.

One funny example, which I came across in the book *Making Marriage Simple*, is the story of a couple in counseling who were supposed to share something they would like their spouse to do in bed. The wife, at first nervous and hesitant to share anything, finally lets it out: "I've always wanted you to suck my big toe." Her husband smiled and happily agreed to make her dream come true. I guess you just never know what can happen until you fess up!

A word of warning here—let's say your spouse's greatest desire involves feet and you just can't do it. The last thing you want to do, after this intimate, embarrassing confession, is to disgustedly say "Ewww! No way!" Think about the effect that response may have the next time your partner considers sharing an idea with you. Try to be open-minded, but if it's simply not your jam, then say so. Just do it gently and respectfully so you don't cause your best friend to clam up forever in this department.

Expressing likes and dislikes is an important way for both partners to feel safe in this extremely vulnerable and intimate experience. Share, listen, be considerate, and as often as possible, express your desires in terms of what you *do* enjoy rather than what you don't. Expressing what you desire will give your partner clarity and confidence in meeting your needs.

Sixth Key Ingredient: Selflessness

Selflessness is probably the single most important thing a spouse can give in any area of marriage, including physical intimacy. The more you can seek your spouse's happiness, the more mutual joy and satisfaction you both will find. Asking yourself "What can I do for my spouse?" rather than "What should my spouse do for me?" will allow for a positive experience for both partners. Though the goal here is not to get your partner to be more willing to give, selflessness is contagious. The more each partner chooses to focus on the other, the more each person will feel loved and able to respond. Put simply, selflessness motivates selflessness. Do whatever you can to fulfill the needs and desires of your spouse, and you will find your spouse more willing to do the same.

If both partners work to create a strong emotional bond, appreciate the importance of a healthy love life, seek to understand differences, remember a slow and affectionate warm-up, communicate openly about needs, and prioritize selflessness, then physical intimacy can be just what it should be: a powerful, bonding, and enjoyable experience.

Two-Minute Action Steps

Consider the quality of your friendship with your spouse. Remember that in order to have great physical intimacy, emotional intimacy is essential. Follow the previous chapters' action steps to strengthen your emotional bond.

Consider how you view the importance of physical intimacy in marriage. Is it a priority for you? Decide to have an attitude of appreciation for this unique and powerful bonding experience.

Talk to your spouse about typical biological differences between men and women when it comes to lovemaking. Consider checking out a few books together to learn more. Remember that a clear understanding of differences can help both partners meet each other's needs.

The next time you initiate a romantic evening with your spouse, set the stage with candlelight, soft music, and plenty of loving affection.

Consider some of the things you would like to experience with your spouse with regard to your love life, and communicate openly.

The next time you have a romantic evening—or morning or afternoon—focus primarily on what you can do for your spouse.

Chapter 8

Fight the Good Fight: Simple Tools for Handling Conflict

An eye for an eye will only make
the whole world blind.

—**Mahatma Gandhi,** INDIAN CIVIL RIGHTS LEADER

In marriage, conflicts are guaranteed to arise from time to time. Consider how many opportunities we have to disagree: how to squeeze the toothpaste, how to roll the toilet paper, how to decorate the house, how to spend the money, how to raise the kids, how to spend the evenings, when to spend time with in-laws, what friends to hang out with and how often, how to spend the holidays, where to go on vacation, what to do for fun, what TV show to watch, who gets the remote control, who goes grocery shopping, who pays the bills, where to go to church, who cleans the toilets, and on and on.

Not only do we have different opinions on how to do life, but we also have different interests and personalities (because we are and always will be different people). Consider some of the personality dichotomies that might make it hard to see eye to eye:

adventurous or homebody, chatty or quiet, frivolous or thrifty, liberal or conservative, early bird or night owl, extrovert or introvert, religious or not religious, and different levels of independence.

Many of these differences are what cause a husband and wife to fall for each other in the first place. He loves how she has so much to share, and she loves that he's such a great listener. She loves how adventurous he is, and he loves how she keeps him grounded. He loves her energy, and she loves his peacefulness. Our differences keep things interesting. Of course, sooner or later, these differences are going to cause conflicts. For Scott and me, our differences didn't affect us as much before marriage because we were still living separate lives in separate places. After we married, we began depending on each other to make life work. Now everything we do affects each other and, let's face it, we're going to disagree.

Disagreements are natural. Many conflicts are ones that won't be solved because they have to do with deep personality differences. In fact, marriage researcher Dr. John Gottman has found that 69 percent of the conflicts in marriage are unsolvable. They are the let's-agree-to-disagree-and-find-a-way-to-live-with-it kind of conflicts. The trick is, spouses need the tools to handle their differences in ways that allow them to understand each other and respectfully come up with solutions. Without those tools, spouses risk creating negativity in the space between them and severing the important connections that hold them close. This chapter will explore some of the tools that can effectively allow spouses to navigate the waters of conflict in marriage while keeping their bond strong.

Start Softly

In Dr. Gottman's four decades of research, he has found that 96 percent of the time, the outcome of a conflict can be determined by how it begins in the first three minutes. If a couple starts a discussion about a problem or conflict in the right way, there's a great chance they will be able to stay respectful and be creative problem solvers. As organizational behavior experts Kerry Patterson, Joseph Grenny, Ron McMillan, and Al Switzler say in their insightful book *Crucial Conversations*, what is so essential in handling conflict is that people feel they are in a safe environment. "If you don't fear that you're being attacked or humiliated," the authors write, "you yourself can hear almost anything and not become defensive." However, if someone starts a conversation with a criticism or attack, the other person will likely feel the need to protect and defend, sending both partners into a downward spiral.

A big part of starting softly has to do with the tone of voice we use, which can either communicate blame and anger or a respectful readiness to explore the problem. My neighbor Dr. Kent Griffiths has counseled couples for more than forty years. As he explained, "The tone of voice we use is so important. The bottom line is creating emotional safety. If someone has a need to confront their partner, they just need to do it in a respectful way."

For example, consider the husband who comes home thirty minutes late for dinner. His wife can greet him by saying, "I can't believe you are this late for dinner! That is so rude!" Of course, she might feel justified in her frustration. However, odds are that starting her discussion this way is going to backfire with a defensive retort from the husband, who could easily respond with something like, "Hey, hold on there now. Don't jump on me like that! It wasn't my fault I was late. My boss kept me late to meet an unexpected deadline. If you would wait for two minutes so I could explain then you would know that!" She may now feel attacked and even more frustrated with his lack of validation.

Now, going back to when the husband first comes in the door, imagine if the wife had said, "Hey, hon! I'm glad you're home. You know, I was expecting you a little while ago. I'm a little frustrated that you're so late. Did something come up?" In that way, she is still expressing that she's frustrated, but she is not attacking or criticizing him, so he doesn't feel like he has to jump to his own defense. In this case, he is more likely to hear that he hurt her and respond with understanding, perhaps with something like, "I'm so sorry I'm late. We had an unexpected deadline come up. I should have called."

When we have a problem to discuss in marriage, the best way to ensure a calm and creative problem-solving conversation is to start the discussion respectfully, without blame or attack. If we can do that, we are well on our way to handling our conflicts with understanding and love.

Seek First to Understand

One of the most important tools in marriage is simply focusing on understanding your spouse's point of view. I love how Steven Covey introduces this concept in his book *The 7 Habits of Highly Effective People* with the story of an eye exam. As he suggests, picture yourself in the office of an optometrist. After listening to you complain for a while, the optometrist takes off his glasses and hands them to you. The conversation goes like this:

> "Put these on," he says. "I've worn this pair of glasses for ten years now, and they've really helped me. I have an extra pair at home; you can wear these."

So you put them on, but it only makes the problem worse.

"This is terrible!" you exclaim. "I can't see a thing!"

"Well, what's wrong?" he asks. "They work great for me. Try harder."

"I am trying," you insist. "Everything is a blur."

"Well, what's the matter with you? Think positively."

"Okay. I positively can't see a thing."

"Boy, are you ungrateful!" he chides. "And after all I've done to help you!"

Isn't it ridiculous? Although it may not be so obvious, this is often what happens in marriage. We are so focused on getting our partner to see things our way that we forget they have their own lenses on. Seeking understanding is key to working out disagreements in any relationship, but it's especially important in marriage because we are so interdependent and our feelings run so deep. We cannot be truly happy in our relationship when we feel our spouse simply doesn't understand our needs. When we take the time and effort to listen to and learn about what is important to our spouse, we can move forward in productive and creative problem solving.

The other day, my mom's husband, Bob, told me about a situation in which his desire to understand his wife was the key to finding a solution to their problem. Bob felt like their cable bill was too high, so he wanted to slash some programs. His first approach with my mom, Susie, "didn't go so well," because he didn't listen to her needs first. He simply explained his desire to lower the cable bill. Afterward, Bob thought to himself, "There's got to be another way to do this. I'm getting resistance, but that's not because Susie is a stubborn person. Something near and dear is getting bumped into."

Bob tried again, seeking to understand her needs first. On the next approach, he asked her what she enjoyed watching and what would be important for her to keep. This sounds so simple, doesn't it? But this tool of seeking understanding can make or break a problem-solving session. When she felt she was in a safe place and he truly wanted to understand her needs, she was able to explain the particular shows that helped her relax or made her laugh—just things she enjoyed after a long day. Once Bob understood that and Susie *felt* understood, he was on safer ground to explore options. She no longer felt threatened and was open to problem solving.

It turns out, they were able to call their cable company and get their bill reduced while keeping all the channels they wanted. Win-win! As Bob explained, "We both got what we wanted. I got to save money, and she got to keep the channels she likes. It wasn't how I first thought we'd solve the problem. If I had done it my way, it wouldn't have worked. I'd have cut off all the wrong branches." What a wise man. He knows that understanding his wife's needs is the first step to creatively solving a problem. (They both chuckled telling me that their other secret is "Happy wife, happy life.") So it goes for any marriage—we can only reach creative solutions when we seek understanding and feel understood.

Use Questions for Clarity

One important action that allows us to gain understanding is asking questions. In the example above, Bob could only discover his wife's needs by asking important questions such as "Why is this important to you?" or "How do you think we should do this?" These questions, although simple, are incredibly powerful. In asking the question, we communicate to our spouse "I care about you, your needs, and your opinions." Not only do questions help the other person know that you care, but the answers to the questions provide meaningful information that fosters understanding.

Consider the wife who comes to her husband and says, "I'd like to get a dog." The husband's first thought is: *No way. I don't like pets. Hair and poop everywhere, extra expense, barking every time I come home. No way.* If he says that right away, is his wife going to feel like her husband cares about her needs and desires? Probably not. They clearly have a problem: she wants a dog and he does not. Whether that problem turns into creative problem solving or a frustrating battle depends very much on whether he decides to explore her needs with questions. If he responds without exploring first, she will likely get frustrated, feeling he doesn't care enough to seek understanding, and the dialogue will not be productive. She will repeat why she wants one, and he will repeat why he doesn't. If, on the other hand, he uses questions for clarity, they will be on their way to creative and respectful problem solving.

He could choose to respond with "You want a dog, huh? Really? What excites you about having a dog?" Because he asked, she has a chance to explain her feelings: "You know, I've been think-ing about this for a long time, and I would just like to feel a little safer at home when you are traveling for work." He hadn't thought about that. This respectful start will help them move into creative problem-solving mode. He can now validate her concerns and seek solutions with her. Whether they decide to get a dog or not, they will both have a chance to explore each other's needs and come up with an answer together, rather than becoming frustrated and entrenched in an argument. Questions are an important tool for setting the stage for respectful dialogue when those inevitable differences arise.

Marriage research shows that unhappily married couples have a tendency to interpret each other's messages in distorted ways, often hearing something that wasn't really there. Have you ever been there? For example, let's say you just got home and poured out the basket of laundry you couldn't get to earlier when your kids come screeching down the stairs, embroiled in a battle that needs your attention. Then the smoke alarm goes off as you realize the rice on the stove is burning. You turn off the stove and run to open the windows to let the smoke out, while your three-year-old finds a marker and starts drawing on the wall. (Yes, I've been there.) You grab the markers, along with a washcloth, trying to remain cool as you show her a more appropriate canvas. Suddenly, the garage door opens and your spouse walks in, excited to see everyone, but then eyes the room and asks, "What happened here?" Your pulse jumping, you translate his message as: "Why can't you get your act together?"

It is all too easy for a spouse to interpret a harmless comment as criticism. Of course, if that spouse feels offended or hurt by such a comment, a conflict is likely to result. Before jumping to conclusions, partners need to take a deep breath and evaluate the situation. Willpower is important here. Before you let yourself react badly to a comment, ask yourself this question: "Is it possible that I am reading this wrong?" In the above example, before she yells at her husband for being so insensitive, this wife could ask herself, "Did he actually suggest that I am being irresponsible and letting things fall apart here, or did he mean something else?" If she's not sure, all she needs to do is ask, calmly if possible. It sounds like this: "Before I react, I would like to ask what you meant by that?" In this case, the husband might say, "Oh, I just noticed the smoke in the room and was wondering what was burning."

Rather than making assumptions, try to clarify your spouse's meaning before you get frustrated by what might be a harmless comment. By using your willpower and pausing your emotional reaction until you clarify with your partner, you can easily prevent needless conflicts.

Reflective Listening

One of the greatest tools for gaining and showing understanding is the ability to reflect what you have heard your partner say. Reflective listening is simply one partner explaining back what he heard his partner say to make sure he has it right. This allows her to either feel validated if the reflection was correct or explain again if there was a misunderstanding. This type of feedback might start, "So what I hear you saying is . . . " Of course, this must be more than a trite repetition of words, which can certainly backfire. If done with a sincere desire to understand, however, the simple act of reflecting can allow for respectful, productive dialogue.

Not too long ago, Scott and I experienced how beneficial reflective listening can be. I don't recall what we were going back and forth about, but I remember feeling frustrated that I had to keep repeating myself. I didn't feel like he understood what I was saying. He would state his point, and I'd go back and re-state mine. So I said to him, "Look, why don't you tell me what you think my perspective is, and I'll tell you what I think your perspective is." It was amazing. He said to me exactly what I had been saying. In that moment, I knew he understood my perspective, and I didn't feel like I had to say anything more. He was equally surprised when I was able to say to him what he was thinking and feeling. For both of us, the experience was validating and rewarding to know the other person really did understand. After that, we were able to accept that we just had a difference of opinion and we moved on with greater shared understanding.

It doesn't need to be as formal as that, where we actually said to each other, "OK, let's try explaining this from the other person's shoes." The next time you find yourself in a disagreement with your spouse, try this exercise. Simply reflect what you hear your spouse saying. If one spouse says, "I don't want to go to the beach this year because it's going to cost too much money," don't jump right into explaining why you disagree. First, show your spouse that you've heard and understand what he said. "So, you're worried about the budget and feel it's too expensive this year? Yeah, I can see that." You don't have to agree. Just let him know you get what he's saying. (And if you don't, try really hard to find something you can relate to.)

It feels simple, doesn't it? In the moment, though, when you really want something and your spouse really wants something else, the tendency is to fight for your side right away. That tendency causes the other person to feel they need to fight for their side. Then we just push each other away. In the end, we often end up with less shared understanding than when we started our dialogue. We become entrenched in our own positions. If we can simply show our spouse we understand by reflecting what we have heard, our spouse will be better able to move forward with productive problem solving.

Validating and Empathizing

Validating your partner's emotion is a key part of respectful conflict communication. As Steven Covey has said, "Most people do not listen with the intent to understand; they listen with the intent to reply. They're either speaking or preparing to speak. They're filtering everything through their own paradigms, reading their autobiography into other people's lives." In marriage, our emotional bond motivates us to love and support each other, especially in hard times. Our first instinct may be to try to fix the problem and move on. However, for anyone to feel understood, they must feel that their partner can listen to, validate, and empathize with their experience.

Recently, Scott and I discovered just how important validating emotions and empathizing can be for a marriage. I was tired and a bit wound up at the end of a long day and started to express some of my frustrations to him. Really, all I wanted was a listening ear and to feel like he cared and understood. Scott thought I needed to be cheered up. So, in response to me telling him about feeling stressed with ten kids—ours, plus some neighbor friends—tearing up the house, he said, "How about telling me something happy from your day?" He, sweetly, was trying to cheer me up by getting me to think about something positive. My interpretation was "I don't really want to hear about your frustrations because I've had a long day, too, and I'd like to do something fun with you." That caused me to get more frustrated because I didn't feel validated. I wanted him, my best friend and confidant, to listen to me vent for two minutes and then say, "That must have been tough." Easy enough, right? Scott ended up frustrated, too, because he just wanted to help, and now here I was going the opposite direction.

This is a common predicament for husband and wife. According to marriage therapists Patricia Love and Dr. Steven Stosny, the most important emotional connection tool is an ability to be in tune with your partner by "stepping into the puddle." Stepping into the puddle is simply allowing yourself to feel whatever your partner is feeling. When one person is experiencing some emotion—be it stress, anxiety, discouragement, sadness, anger, or frustration—if her partner is able to swim in the emotions with her a bit and offer support, then both people can step out of the puddle together, much faster than if he tries to just drag her out. The trick is suspending the desire to pull her out of the puddle until she is ready to step out, too. The result of swimming in and stepping out of the puddle together is a loving and bonding experience.

Men and women are slightly different in their need for empathy and support. While both need to feel that their spouse "gets" them and is there for them, women are more likely to need their man "in the puddle" for a bit of venting. They are more likely to need someone to listen. As Love and Stosny suggest, "Be there with her. Don't ignore it; don't 'fix' it, tell her what to do, or try to drag her out of it. If you're just there with her a short time, the two of you can usually step out of the puddle together." Men, on the other hand, might be more likely to need a physical gesture of comfort, like a hug or arm around the shoulder, which communicates that his wife is on his side. Men are also more likely to simply need understanding when they are ready to move on without talking much more about it.

For both husband and wife, the important thing is to step inside each other's shoes. Try to understand the needs and emotions of your spouse, suspending your own desires and judgments. Validating those emotions and showing that you understand will build loving and lasting connections.

It's Not You; It's Me

When discussing a conflict, where we place the simple, tiny words "I" and "you" makes a big difference in the response we are likely to receive. Consider the different feeling in these messages: "You are late for dinner again" versus "I feel frustrated when you are late for dinner." It may seem subtle, but the reaction to each statement is measurably different in marriage and communication research. As human beings, we don't like to be challenged or criticized. We don't like to be accused of doing something wrong, even if we are technically guilty. Something about it just doesn't feel good, and our natural response is to protect ourselves by explaining why it wasn't our fault. That's why a statement like "You are late" is likely to cause the reaction of "Well, let me explain why it's not my fault," which may or may not appease the person who is upset. On the other hand, a statement that starts with, "I feel . . . " might welcome more understanding. You can't argue with what someone else is feeling. That's not a stated fact; it's just a description of an experience. A husband or wife who starts an explanation with "I think" or "I feel" is more likely to help their spouse focus on their emotional needs rather than on defending himself or herself.

This goes for any conflict issue that arises in marriage. "You left the car without gas, and now I'm going to be late for work" versus "I'm frustrated that the car has no gas because now I'm going to be late for work." Or "You went over on our grocery budget again" versus "I'm nervous about our grocery spending." Or "You have been spending too much time at your parents' house" versus "I would really like it if you were home more often." Starting the conversation with "I" in these situations allows the listener to focus on the needs of the other person—he or she is frustrated or unhappy about something. When the sentences start with "You," on the other hand, the listener is more likely to immediately consider how to explain or defend why the car doesn't have gas or why the grocery bill is so high. Explanations are important, but first we must come to understand and validate our partner's feelings. When we start our messages with "I," our partner will be more likely to listen and seek understanding.

Body Language

The other night, I was saying something to my son while he was playing with his Legos at our kitchen table. It wasn't about anything terribly important, but it was something I needed to communicate to him. For him, Legos are powerful distractions, easily more interesting than Mom. He occasionally said, "Uh-huh," but he kept looking at those Legos. I finally nudged him and said, "Hey, you. Did you know that you don't just listen with your ears? What else makes you a good listener?" He got the message and stopped what he was doing to give me his attention until I had conveyed my message.

In marriage, too, our body language communicates whether we are interested and concerned or not. (I touched on this in Chapter 5.) Our body language speaks loudly on our behalf and can often reveal whether or not a listening spouse is truly engaged and interested. Consider the difference between the following two situations: First, a husband is telling his wife about a frustrating project at work while she is rummaging around the kitchen. She is listening with her ears, but she isn't looking at him and seems engaged doing her own thing. Or, second, that same husband is telling his wife about the same frustrating issue, and she senses his emotion and sits down at the table to look at him and nods to show her understanding. Can you imagine the different feeling of support the husband receives in the second scenario?

The next time you enter into a conflict discussion with your spouse, remember that body language matters and pay attention to what your body is saying. Are you rolling your eyes or folding your arms or looking elsewhere? If so, research shows that you are likely to communicate to your spouse that you think what they have to say is unimportant, silly, or even crazy. A spouse who gets that message is unlikely to feel validated, understood, or listened to, which will probably cause frustration.

On the other hand, open and positive body language can go a long way in facilitating creative and respectful dialogue. Looking your partner in the eye, having arms opened and relaxed, smiling, turning toward your partner, and nodding to show your attention and understanding all convey the message, "I care what you have to say." That feeling is key to establishing a loving connection during any conversation.

Say What You Mean

Couples can save themselves a great deal of frustration and miscommunication by simply saying exactly what they mean rather than hoping their spouse will pick up on clues. According to John Gray, author of *Men Are from Mars, Women Are from Venus*, women in particular often speak in generalities rather than specifics when they want something and then are frustrated when their husbands don't understand. Indeed, Dr. Gray reports that the most common complaint from wives is that they don't feel heard. That's usually because their husbands heard what they *said* and not what they *meant*. If she says, "We never go out," he'll probably start explaining how they just went out last weekend. That explanation will likely make her feel frustrated that he doesn't "get" her. What she meant was "I don't feel like I've gotten enough time with you lately, and I'd like to go out." Or, if she says, "Honey, it sure is hot in here," he may very likely respond with, "The thermostat says 68." What she meant was "Could you please turn on the fan because I'm uncomfortable?" He didn't hear that. Frustrated, she starts thinking what a doofus her husband is and how he just isn't concerned about her needs.

Women, do yourselves a favor: if you need something from your spouse, be clear. Say what you mean. Men, if your wife is being vague, do yourselves a favor and try to read between the lines. If you want a date with your husband, then say, "I'd love to go out on a date with you this weekend." If you are cold, try saying, "Honey, I'm cold. Would you mind handing me that blanket?" Bingo. He's happy to help. He *wants* to be the man who fulfills your needs. It's a simple way to come to mutual understanding—say what you mean. Don't expect your spouse to guess it right, and don't assume they should know you well enough to know everything you're thinking.

Say What You Do Want

In marriage, it's easy for spouses to get frustrated about a few things along the way. Actually, we can all count on getting frustrated about lots of things along the way. That's the nature of intimate relationships. Often, when spouses recognize something they don't like, it comes out that way: "I don't like it when . . . " or "I don't want . . . " Though these are still "I" messages (which I mentioned are a better way to state feelings than "you" messages), these statements are framed in a negative way. Such negative framing can cause tension in the space between you and your spouse. Much more likely to build a path to a positive solution is saying what you *do* want. So, rather than saying, "I don't like it when you leave the lawn like that," she might try, "I really appreciate having a nicely mowed lawn. Can we make that happen?" He just got a kind and direct clue about what would make his spouse happy rather than a complaint about what doesn't. Or, rather than "I don't like it when you paint the walls without talking to me," he might try, "I would appreciate it if you talked to me before making a big decision like that." Now she knows what he wants and needs.

This kind of open and positive communication is key in healthy relationships. As family therapist Terrence Real writes in his book *The New Rules of Marriage: A Breakthrough Program For 21st-Century Relationships*, "You cannot create an extraordinary relationship unless you're willing to do the hard work of identifying what it is that you want and pursuing it. You cannot sustain a great relationship without taking risks. Too many of us are afraid of rocking the boat . . . and so we 'compromise,' trying to make peace with what we see as our partner's limitations. This common outcome woefully sells short both you and your partner."

My neighbor Carol told me how speaking up about her needs helped her navigate one particular conflict. For years, she had done the grocery shopping. At some point, her husband started mentioning that she was spending too much. She didn't like that. To solve the problem, she said, "OK, I'd like you to do the shopping, and I'll do the cooking." Ever since that day, her husband has done all the shopping for their family of thirteen! Can you imagine if Carol had just quietly fumed over her husband's finance tips? Or kept telling him that she didn't like his advice? That would have just caused more stress, and now they both agree, "It's just not worth it!" She came up with a creative solution and let her husband know what she wanted.

It is so much easier to do something you know your spouse wants rather than to *not* do something he or she *doesn't* want. If it drives you crazy when your spouse leaves his dish on the table, remind him how much you appreciate it when everyone clears their dish. Don't just complain about the dirty dish. It sounds simple, but do you feel the difference? Using a positive approach is more likely to motivate while still keeping the feeling of love between you.

Consider Timing

Think about the times when your spouse is tired, hungry, or stressed. Those probably aren't the best times to bring up a problem. Our body's physical needs have a way of overpowering our emotional capabilities. For example, Scott is a morning person. He pretty much always wakes up around 5:30 a.m., whether he wants to or not. By the end of the day, he's exhausted. If I have something I need to discuss with him, a problem, or even a scheduling question, I know that discussion will go ten times better if I wait until morning.

This is the language you can use to make sure your spouse is ready to engage, according to family therapist Kent Griffiths: "Hey, there's something I want to talk to you about. Are you in a good place?" If not, you can simply say, "OK, let me know when you're ready to talk." An awareness of pacing, as Dr. Griffiths explained to me, helps both people be ready to jump into discussion and keep communication respectful. By choosing a time to talk when our spouse is rested, fed, refreshed, and ready, we increase our chances of having a positive dialogue. If you're not sure whether your spouse is up for a chat, just ask.

Take a Break

My kids know that when they have broken an important rule, they will earn a little "time out" in their room. Mostly this exercise is just to give them some physical space where they can think things over for a few minutes and calm down if they're upset. Typically, they come out with a new perspective and are ready to face the world again. The same need arises in marriage conflicts. Sometimes we just need to step away to gain some clarity. Arguing while emotions

are running high actually moves blood away from the brain—wh
we need it most—and sends it to our arms and legs, preparing us
to fight or flee. This tendency may have had more purpose in our
caveman days, when we relied more on our physical capacities to
stay alive. Luckily, our brains have evolved and we can better reason
through our problems, if we can just calm down. When emotions
are running high, the best thing we can do is take a break.

Early in our marriage, Scott was good at this, and I was not. I
preferred to "fight it out," which usually meant debating something
when neither of us were in a good place to communicate. Over the
years, I've come to appreciate that when one of us starts feeling
frustrated during our conversation, we can simply say, "I need a
break." That gives us a chance to calm down, get some perspective,
think over what each of us is trying to say, and come back to try
again. Usually, the second time around, we solve whatever the issue
was fairly quickly and easily because we stopped the downward
spiral of negative emotion.

It's natural for the less mature parts of our personality to come
out when we are frustrated. That's why it's so important to take
space and get back in control. Family therapist Terrence Real calls
it easing the "child" inside us. He suggests, "When immature parts
of your personality become triggered—either the wounded, over-
whelmed part of you or the defensive, entitled part—in your mind's
eye, take that child in your lap, put your arms around him, love him
. . . and take his sticky hands off the steering wheel."

Talk with your spouse about the idea of taking a breather. Agree
beforehand that when you start feeling like emotions are running
too high to continue in a productive conversation, you will both
take a break. If either spouse requests a break, both partners must
agree to respect the request. This does not mean that you don't
want to solve the problem or that you don't care about how the
other person is feeling, be it angry, irritated, or exasperated. It sim-

ply means, "I care about you so much that I want to move forward calmly and respectfully. I'm not in a place to do that right now, so I need a short break to gather my thoughts." If you both can have a mutual understanding that this is what "taking a break" is all about, hopefully respecting the request will be easy. Agree ahead of time what your phrase or signal will be, and agree that the person who needed a break will come back when ready. This simple tool can keep many disagreements from spiraling out of control. Taking a breather can help you both get back on track to find mutual understanding and positive solutions.

Let It Go

As noted previously, according to marriage researcher John Gottman, 69 percent of conflicts in marriage are unending and unavoidable because they relate to basic personality differences. That's a big chunk of disagreements! But it makes sense when you consider all the little differences between two people. He likes to squeeze the toothpaste in the middle; she likes the end. She likes to stay up late; he likes to go to bed early. He likes fish and vegetables for dinner; she likes pasta. He loves the mountains; she loves the beach. She's thrifty; he thinks budgets are confining. Living together happily is going to require some compromise, some give and take. There are going to be some conflicts that we just can't resolve. We have to agree to disagree or simply let it go. If I get to the toothpaste first, I'm going to squeeze in the middle. Thankfully, even though he's a roll-up-from-the-end-of-the-tube kind of guy, Scott doesn't complain. The important questions to ask yourself are: Is bringing this up going to change anything? Is it going to benefit our relationship? If not, then let it go.

Of course, you can't sweep your emotions under the rug if they really still bother you. If you do that, you might just explode at some point over something trivial. If something bothers you repeatedly, as counselor Dr. Jamie Turdorf suggests, then it's important to talk about it. If it's important, then bring it up. But first, take a step back and ask yourself whether this issue might not bother you at all after a good night's rest or a deep breath. If it's something you can live with, then let it go.

In those times when you have experienced conflict and emotions are running high, do what you can to cool down quickly afterward. Researchers at UC Berkeley have found that, especially for wives, the ability to let go of anger after an argument is correlated with marital happiness. Psychologist Lian Block, who led the study, explains, "Emotions such as anger and contempt can seem very threatening for couples. But our study suggests that if spouses, especially wives, are able to calm themselves, their marriages can continue to thrive." That might sound obvious, but think about your last argument with your spouse. It can be all too easy to hold on to feelings of resentment and frustration, even righteous indignation, when we feel we've been wronged. Do yourself a favor next time and remember that holding on to those feelings will only do a disservice to your marriage.

Gratitude

Many marriage studies show that one thing is significantly more powerful than nagging, criticizing, sulking, or complaining in motivating changes in behavior: gratitude. If your spouse is doing (or not doing) something that is driving you crazy, try an experiment. Rather than pestering your spouse about that behavior, find something to be grateful for and thank your spouse.

Consider the example of the wife who had nagged her husband

for months to paint the bedroom. He hadn't done it, causing her mounds of frustration. However, when she stopped pushing him and tried thanking him for the little things he did well, within three weeks, he found a way to get the bedroom painted.

As Dr. John Gottman said in an interview with *The Atlantic*, "There's a habit of mind that the [marriage] masters have, which is this: they are scanning social environment for things they can appreciate and say thank you for. They are building this culture of respect and appreciation very purposefully. Disasters are scanning the social environment for partners' mistakes."

"It's not just scanning environment," chimed in Julie Gottman. "It's scanning the partner for what the partner is doing right or scanning him for what he's doing wrong and criticizing versus respecting him and expressing appreciation."

Imagine the difference in the atmosphere of a marriage when both people are regularly looking for what their partner is doing well. When we feel appreciated, we are so much more likely to want to work with our spouse and find solutions to problems. It's not about always getting what we want; it's about working together in a way that motivates each partner to enjoy making the other person happy. I like how marriage therapist Dr. John Chapman put it: "The object of love is not getting something you want but doing something for the well-being of the one you love. It is a fact, however, that when we receive affirming words, we are far more likely to be motivated to reciprocate."

Thank your spouse regularly for the little things, whether it's taking out the trash, driving the kids to school, sweeping the walkway, reading bedtime stories every night, or going to work so faithfully. You might be surprised to find how motivated your partner becomes to earn more of your praise and gratitude.

Think Win-Win

In life, we are often taught to believe that in order for someone to win, someone has to lose. In school competitions, there is usually a winner, which means everyone else doesn't win. In sports, we want our team to win. In board games, someone has to come in first or take all the money or be the last one standing. In marriage, it's easy to keep the same attitude, but marriage is not a board game.

When my future father-in-law was vetting me at dinner one night a few weeks before I was going to marry his son, he asked me a question. "If one day you want to paint the walls red, and Scott wants to paint them white, what would you do?" Um, think quick. Red . . . white . . . "Paint them pink!" I said. He laughed. I felt pretty clever. I suppose that was a better answer than "Well, I would still paint them all red because that's what I want!" No, I wasn't going to be selfish. But really? Pink? There had to be a better answer.

Compromise plays a role in every marriage, but compromising doesn't have to mean that no one gets what they really want. Compromise can either be done in an adversarial way or in a collaborative way. Adversarial compromise is like two people sitting on opposite sides of a table, hashing their way to a deal. Wife is saying, "I want to go to the beach for four days with our family. Each night at the hotel is $100, so that will cost $400." Husband, on the opposite side, is saying "That's too much. I don't think we should spend any money. Our budget is tight right now." She says, "Well, I really want to get away. Tell you what, I'll cut it down to two days so it won't cost so much. $200. Final offer." He's still uncomfortable with spending that much, but he knows he has to give somewhere. "Deal." She gets part of what she wants and he isn't as uncomfortable in the end as he could have been.

A collaborative approach, on the other hand, is when husband

and wife work together to get what both people really want with a win-win ending. It just takes a little more creative problem solving. Picture husband and wife sitting on the same side of the table, analyzing the variables in front of them. What she really wants is four days away at the beach with the family. He is uncomfortable spending money. They brainstorm a bit and come up with a win-win solution that neither of them had originally come to the table with: camping at the beach for four days! He's happy to not spend money on a hotel, and she's happy to get a few days at the beach. This is exactly what Scott and I came up with for our spring break this year. We both got what we wanted but in a different way than we were originally thinking.

When you have a problem to solve, think creatively. Don't try to win alone. As Dr. Griffiths said to me, in marriage, if you win (at the expense of your spouse), you lose intimacy and you lose closeness. In short, "If you win, you lose." Go into your problem solving with a commitment to collaborate. Thinking win-win will open the door to many creative possibilities and allow you to resolve conflicts productively. For the paint question, I don't think pink was the right answer. Now I would probably say, "If we sat down and talked about it for a while, I'm sure we could find a way to leave some walls white and paint some walls red." We might even decide, in the end, that plan was our favorite way to go anyway. Sometimes you just have to think outside the box (or the room, or the budget).

Conflict in marriage is inevitable. If you handle it well, you can creatively solve your problems, keep the feeling of love in the space between you, and avoid the trouble that comes when conflict communication goes wrong.

TWO-MINUTE ACTION STEPS

(COMPLETE ONCE AND REPEAT OFTEN):

If you have a problem to address with your spouse, remember to bring it up softly, without attacking and without anger. Remember that the first few minutes can make or break the path of a conflict discussion.

When your spouse brings up a problem, before explaining how you feel, remember to first seek understanding. Ask yourself whether you clearly understand what your spouse is trying to communicate.

When your spouse brings up a problem and your first instinct is to disagree, or when you don't understand something your spouse is doing, ask questions to clarify.

The next time your spouse is explaining his or her side of a problem, use reflective listening to show your spouse you have heard and understood.

If your spouse is upset, show empathy. Validate emotions by letting your spouse know you understand or can imagine how that must feel. Let your spouse feel that you are there in that emotional space with them before seeking to pull him or her out.

Rather than attacking your spouse when you are frustrated, use "I" messages to explain how you feel and to help prevent defensiveness.

Be aware of your body language the next time you are having a conflict discussion with your spouse. Ask yourself if your body language is communicating openness and concern or closed-off irritability.

When you need something from your spouse, say what you need directly. Don't assume your spouse should know.

Rather than saying what you don't like or don't want, tell your spouse what you do like and do want. Remember that this can make the difference between a spouse who feels criticized and a spouse who is motivated to change.

Talk with your spouse about a phrase that means "I need a break" during a conflict, and agree to respect the request whenever it is made. The next time you start feeling angry during a conflict, remember that moving forward in anger may cause you to do or say something you will regret. Take a break.

The next time you have a potential conflict to address, remember to collaborate by thinking win-win rather than win-lose. If you do, there is a better chance that a creative solution can be found.

Chapter 9

Do Not Try This at Home: Bitter Behaviors That Take a Big Bite

If you want to sacrifice the admiration of many men
for the criticism of one, go ahead, get married.

—**Katherine Hepburn,**

AMERICAN ACTRESS

As the previous chapter points out, conflict is normal and inevitable in marriage. That's just what happens when two interesting people join separate lives into one. Conflict isn't bad in and of itself, but some behaviors used in conflict are more hurtful than helpful. Indeed, as I read recently from Jenny Erikson on the blog *The Stir*, tiny behaviors can add up to crushing defeat for a marriage. In her case, she called it quits after eleven years—even though, as she describes, "he never hit me, didn't call me names, and I have no reason to believe another woman was involved. . . . The only way I know how to describe it is death by a thousand cuts." Jenny goes on to describe that even though there were no major breakdowns, the little things gone wrong were enough to destroy her relationship.

By removing these behaviors completely, you can keep your

marriage loving even when you have problems to solve. Here are a few simple suggestions of what *not* to do.

Don't Sweat the Small Stuff

In life, and marriage, most stuff is small stuff. You know: toilet paper put on the "wrong" way, dirty socks on the floor, someone coming home late, dinner that didn't get made, too many nights at the in-laws', someone hogging the covers, or a comment taken the wrong way. You can let it get to you, or you can let it go. If it really bothers you, and it's an ongoing issue, then talk to your spouse about it. No one wants to blow a fuse due to too much bottledup frustration. But if you can take a step back and ask, "Is this really important?" you might find that you can let a lot more go than you think.

For a time, many therapists took the approach that venting was good for anger. As it turns out, anger really just begets more anger. Expressing yourself is one thing. Letting yourself fume at your partner over something trivial can be damaging to those loving connections that hold you together. Scott once lived with a friend who dealt remarkably well with the frustrations of life. Once, Scott asked him, "How do you stay so calm?" The roommate said, "I just take a deep breath and try to think about something else. Usually after ten minutes, whatever it was doesn't seem to matter anymore." That sort of attitude can go a long way in marriage.

For my friend Mariah, something as mundane as sorting the mail brings an opportunity for her husband to communicate love by what he doesn't do. As she put it, "I tend to let the mail pile up. Instead of asking me why I can't get my act together and sort the mail, when the pile becomes unbearable, Evan simply goes through it and takes care of it, leaving anything essential for me to see out for my review. I appreciate feeling like someone has my back and is tolerant of areas where I have room for improvement." Mariah's husband could have let a little thing like that get under his skin. But he knows it's just not worth it (and he probably knows she never signed up to be the official mail sorter in the family). Either way, finding ways to let those little things go rather than getting irritated can be a source of strength in marriage.

Don't Make Assumptions

Isn't it easy to come up with our own explanations for why our partner said or did something? Unfortunately, those assumptions are often negative, and they are often wrong. As human beings, we have the tendency to make ourselves into victims, especially if a behavior has a history. For example, the other night, Scott came home thirty minutes late when I was counting on him for dinner. He goes to the gym at the end of his workday, so I immediately jumped in, saying, "Scott, the gym should not be more important than your family! I need you here!" Of course, if I had given him a little space and asked him what had come up, he would have been able to tell me that he had gotten wrapped up in an important phone call with a client and hadn't even had the chance to go to the gym. Whoops.

One scene in the movie *Father of the Bride* demonstrates how assumptions can cause trouble. Annie, the soon-to-be bride, opens a gift from her fiancé. The gift is a blender. She fumes and breaks off the engagement, assuming her man clearly expects her to be a domestic champion, mixing up masterpieces in the kitchen all day long. Her father, in a rare moment of patience and perspective, calms her down, saying, "He just thought you might want to blend something, that's all." She smiles, realizing she had jumped to con-clusions. In no time, the wedding is back on.

There are dozens of opportunities to make assumptions in marriage every day. Whether it's assuming why he's irritable, assuming she's happy to go bowling for date night again, assuming he would like the lime green paint in the bathroom, or assuming her silence means she didn't like dinner, we can easily get frustrated over nothing. In marriage and anything else, if you assume, you are setting yourself up for trouble. Here's a simple solution: when in doubt, just ask.

Don't criticize

Marriage researcher John Gottman has found in his decades of studying couples that one of the first signs of marriage distress is the presence of criticism. Complaining about a behavior isn't necessarily a bad thing . . . as long as it's directed at an isolated situation or a particular behavior. For example, if a husband has left his laundry on the floor, his wife might say, "That really bothers me when you leave your clothes there." That's a complaint. A criticism would be saying "You are so lazy" and attacking her spouse's character. When spouses start criticizing each other, their marriage is in trouble. The connections that typically help tie two people together in that intimate bond are being broken with words alone. Saying things like "You can't do anything right" or "What is wrong with you?" creates harmful negativity and distance.

If you have a problem to discuss, bring it up softly and respectfully rather than with criticism. If bringing it up probably won't change anything because it's one of those character differences or an irregular occurrence, try to handle it with patience and understanding. In marriage, that practice of patience builds ironclad connections. As my friend Melissa put it, "Greg makes me feel like I am still so wonderful, even if I haven't done the dishes that day.

Instead of complaining when he comes home that they're not done, he does them himself without me even needing to ask or apologize. He will also do that with the laundry. Lately he has been saying, 'I am on your team, and we help each other out.' Then he kisses me and gets to work. I love that husband of mine." It's easy to see why. Most people aren't criticized into changing. Love, on the other hand, is a powerful force for good.

Don't Get Defensive

It is part of human nature to want to defend ourselves when we feel we are being attacked. The problem is, this tendency can set us up for trouble and keep us from hearing when our partner has a real concern. Defensiveness is a behavior that Dr. Gottman believes is so poisonous to marriage that its frequent use can be a predictor of future divorce. Defensiveness is really just a way of blaming your partner for the problem he or she brought up, which typically escalates the conflict rather than solving anything.

Consider this example: A husband says to his wife, "I think we need to cut down on the shoe shopping." She responds defensively with "Hey, I'm not the only one spending around here. Look at the big-screen TV you just purchased. Did we really need that many inches?" Rather than trying to understand his concern, she turned the problem back on him. That kind of reaction is worse than simply not solving the original problem. It escalates the problem to a new level.

Many times in our marriage, I have become defensive when Scott has simply been trying to tell me something that has frustrated him. I was taking it personally when he just meant it as helpful, and important, feedback. After all, we have to be able to communicate with each other when a problem surfaces. He falls into the trap, too, sometimes stopping to defend himself if he hears me saying something related to his behavior. Becoming defensive is unhelpful on every level, limiting our abilities to listen and learn. The trick is to lower our guard, quiet our pride, and be open to our partner's needs.

Don't Withdraw

Another behavior that causes a great deal of trouble is what Dr. Gottman calls "stonewalling," which is when a spouse starts tuning out or withdrawing from a conflict discussion. This is different from taking a short break to cool down. Withdrawing is closing up, ending the discussion, and communicating—whether it's intentional or not—that "figuring this out with you is not important to me."

Dr. Gottman has found that men are often the first to withdraw in a conflict, usually when they feel their spouse is nagging or attacking them. According to science, this withdrawal mechanism is likely part of our ancient chemistry. When our primitive ancestors came across a wild beast, for example, the desire to flee had life-saving purpose. Wild beasts aren't normally part of life anymore (even on your spouse's worst day), but uncomfortable situations can still bring out the same urge to escape. Unfortunately, that very mechanism might be the numberone cause for failed marriages, since a husband withdrawing sends a message to his wife that he doesn't care, escalating her frustration, which escalates his withdrawal in a vicious cycle.

Withdrawing can happen with or without leaving the room. If a spouse isn't using typical verbal cues like "uh-huh," head nods, questions, eye contact, or other feedback, the person has likely withdrawn, both physically and emotionally, from the conversation. Essentially, the person has tuned out, signaling a lack of interest in the problem at hand. That, in turn, communicates a lack of concern for the spouse searching for help.

Rather than escaping the problem, withdrawing makes the problem worse. Being present during times of conflict is an important signal that you care. Even if your spouse is not coming to you with the most appealing communication style (for example, it feels nagging or critical), try to see past the exterior to the real concern he or she is trying to express. If she's speaking in a way that is making it hard for you to listen, let her know, and lovingly ask her if she can try again in a way that will help you understand what she needs. We all want to know our spouse is on our side. Be available to discuss problems when they arise if you want to keep your marital bond strong. Don't just duck for cover.

Don't Respond When You're Angry

Trying to resolve a problem when we are angry is like trying to put together a puzzle blindfolded. As mentioned earlier, when we are angry, we don't even have the necessary amount of blood flowing to our brain to solve anything. Rather than reaching agreement, we are more likely to do or say something we'll regret if we continue. Anger is the catalyst for some of the worst behaviors in marriage communication, including yelling, name-calling, and verbal or physical abuse. No one in their right mind wants to use those hurtful behaviors on their spouse. That's why cooling down is so essential. As marriage counselor Dr. William Harley writes, "When spouses are angry with each other, they should say absolutely nothing until they've had a chance to cool off because whatever they say will be abusive—and insane. Yes, insane. Take it from me, a clinical psychologist, when people are angry, they are experiencing temporary insanity and should say nothing until their anger subsides."

Have you ever been there? Have you ever caught yourself going around in circles arguing and then, finally, when you give yourself some space and let the dust settle, you realize you were overreacting? Or you realize that what your spouse was saying isn't *that* ridiculous? In my experience, sometimes all it takes is a few minutes in another room. Then, most of the time, whatever I was frustrated about doesn't seem to matter so much and whatever Scott was saying makes a lot more sense. When you feel yourself getting angry, take a time-out and cool off before continuing. You will be much more likely to come to a productive resolution.

Don't Say "Always" and "Never" (in Negative Ways)

This is a rule I use with my kids all the time. When I hear "She *always* breaks my Legos!" or "He *never* wants to play with me!" I remind them that those statements are just not true. I also remind them that they are welcome to use those words in positive ways, as in "I'll *always* love you" and "I *never* want to hurt your feelings again." But when spoken negatively, "always" and "never" are words that just push two people apart.

The same rule applies in marriage. When we start throwing out negative absolutes to make our point, such as "You are *always* late!" or "You *never* care about what I think!" we are setting ourselves up for a fight. In our anger or frustration, sometimes we like to use these words for dramatic effect. But the fact is, they are not helpful words. Our spouse will only hear the words that make our statement impossible. Rather than trying to work out the problem productively, they will get to work explaining how it's simply not true that they are "always" late or "never" care.

Much more helpful is going back to those "I" and "you" messages, explaining how a certain behavior makes us feel. In this case, it would be much more helpful to say "I'm frustrated that you are late again" or "Sometimes I feel like you don't care what I think." Do you notice the difference? Those descriptive statements of feeling are much more likely to trigger a desire to empathize and resolve the problem than when we use dramatic attacks.

Don't Compare

Telling your husband how great so-and-so's husband is at mowing the lawn or telling your wife that she sounds just like her mother is not likely to be motivating. Indeed, it's more likely to cause your spouse to feel frustrated and perhaps even resentful. Steer clear of comparisons.

I've made the mistake of doing this once or twice. During different periods in our marriage, I have wanted more help at bedtime from Scott (who is often just plain worn out at the end of the day, especially when he worked as an attorney). Occasionally I would say something like, "Did you know that Mr. X does all the bath time, pajamas, brushing teeth, and story time every night? Isn't that great? So nice for his wife!" I hoped to make it clear what other dads did, in case maybe Scott didn't realize that's what he was supposed to do, too (at least that's what I wanted him to do).

Unfortunately for both of us, that approach usually caused him to get frustrated and explain all the things he does that other dads don't do. Neither of us ended up feeling very happy. He didn't feel my gratitude, and I didn't get the help I was looking for. I've since learned to simply tell Scott when I need something from him and to focus on all the things he does for our family that I am grateful for. Scott always prioritizes spending time with our little family.

I am grateful for that. The point is, in the comparison game, you never, ever win. You only see the good things that someone else has rather than the good things that you have. If you need or want something from your spouse, then ask.

Don't Keep Score

Do you have a figurative scorecard that you mark in red every time your spouse makes a mistake? Do you wave that card around whenever another problem comes up? Do you continue to remember follies from the past, even when your spouse has tried to make things right? In marriage, we all make mistakes. We're only human. When we choose to keep score, regularly recalling the mistakes of our spouse or holding a grudge, we're playing a game no one can win. Here's an important rule to help keep the playing field level—don't keep score. If you can work out mistakes in isolation, you'll have a much easier time moving past them.

For example, say a husband forgets his wife's birthday. Yes, that's pretty bad. But if he has apologized and it was just a crazy, busy time in their life and he has tried to make things right, then she needs to let it go. If six months later he forgets to fill the car up with gas on his way home like she asked, it's not fair for her to say, "Yeah, you forgot my birthday, too!"

Marriage research suggests that the ability to forgive and forget is a strong predictor of marital success. In a long-term marriage study, Dr. John Gottman and his colleagues were able to predict with 94 percent accuracy which couples would still be together and which couples would separate after three years based solely on how the couples looked back at events in their past. If they had positive, loving feelings about their history and experiences together, the couples stayed together. If they looked back with feelings of frustration and negativity, they were more likely to separate. Keep in mind, this was all in their heads! It's not that life was easy for some couples and other couples were dealing with real problems. The difference was in whether or not they were able to let their frustrations go. The impact was in their feelings, thoughts, and memories. Keeping score? That's bound to have the wrong impact. The ability to forgive, forget, and move on with loving feelings and hope for the future is vital.

These bitter, destructive behaviors have the potential to take a big bite out of your marital happiness. They won't solve the problems that inevitably come around, and they will dampen the loving feelings you want to keep bright. Leave these behaviors behind whenever you interact with your spouse. If you do, you will find that solving your conflicts, rather than pushing you apart, can actually bring you closer.

TWO-MINUTE ACTION STEPS

(COMPLETE ONCE AND REPEAT OFTEN):

If you feel yourself getting upset by something your spouse is or isn't doing, take a moment to consider if you are "sweating the small stuff." If it's something that probably won't bother you in an hour, or if it's a character trait you probably can't change, then let it go.

The next time you feel yourself about to be offended by something your spouse has done, check whether you are making assumptions. If you are, stop and clarify with your spouse before you come to a conclusion.

If you feel the urge to criticize your spouse for something you don't like, stop. Find a way to calmly, softly explain your feelings about a specific situation or behavior without attacking.

The next time you feel the desire to defend yourself, stop and listen to what your spouse is trying to say. Listen for the feelings and the problem itself, remembering that defensiveness does not help problem solving.

If you feel the urge to withdraw from a conversation with your spouse, stop and remind yourself that you want your spouse's happiness. Listen openly and willingly, no matter how your spouse is communicating, so you can seek a resolution together. If you need a short break to cool down, ask for one, and let your spouse know you'll be back when you are ready to talk.

If you feel yourself getting angry in a conflict situation, ask your spouse for a short break before you continue. Get control, and then try again.

Rather than telling your spouse they "always" or "never" do something, stop and rephrase in a way that is realistic and that captures the way you feel without absolutes.

Rather than comparing your spouse to someone else in an attempt to motivate or make a point, simply remind yourself of what you are grateful for. If you need something, tell your spouse in a kind and loving way after expressing your gratitude.

If your spouse has apologized for a mistake and made a sincere attempt to make things right, don't keep score or bring it up again. Forget it and let it go.

Chapter 10

Making Things Right: Apologies and forgiveness

To be wronged is nothing, unless
you continue to remember it.

—**Confucius,** Chinese philosopher

Within marriage, each partner is constantly impacting the other, which means that there are bound to be plenty of opportunities to apologize and forgive. These two simple phrases are powerful forces for healing in any relationship: "I am sorry" and "I forgive you." Of course, for the words to work, attitude is everything. They must be sincerely expressed with honest intent to repair and move forward.

Apologies and forgiveness are yin and yang in marriage—they are connected and dependent on each other for real healing. If one person apologizes and the other doesn't forgive, then negativity remains. The same is true if one person is willing to forgive but the other refuses to apologize. The forgiver may remain stoic for a time, but if offenses continue without apology, resentment is bound to take root. If both partners are fully committed to making things right when they have gone wrong, then the rough patches in marriage can stay in the past. Apologies and forgiveness, used together, pave the way for a smooth road ahead.

The Art of Apologizing

Part of saying "I'm sorry" is having a willingness to acknowledge that we have done something to hurt our spouse and we have a desire to make things right. According to psychologist Susan Heitler, to fully apologize, a person should follow these steps:

1. Acknowledge the mistake.
2. Express regret.
3. Clarify what was not intentional.
4. Explain the circumstances.
5. Repair the damage.
6. Learn from the mistake and make a plan to prevent the problem in the future

Surely those steps apply to egregious errors between partners as well as smaller blunders. For example, I can recall plenty of times in our marriage when Scott and I have gotten into a disagreement and I've spoken to him with a harsh tone. I know perfectly well that the tone with which we communicate affects the feelings of love and peace in marriage. Scott and I have agreed to either work things out respectfully or take a break until we can. Sometimes that's harder than it sounds. When I've slipped up and communicated in a way that is not respectful, I always know I should apologize. It's strange how difficult that can be. A sincere apology means I was wrong. I don't like being wrong.

One of the great things about marriage is that it simply does not matter who is right and who is wrong. Indeed, most of the time, both people can find something to apologize for anyway. As I often tell my kids, "It takes two to tango." Someone just has to be big enough to go first. It's easier when you remember that what matters most is your relationship. As I mentioned before, the way Dr. Griffiths puts it is: "In marriage, if you win, you lose." If you want to "win" even at the expense of your spouse, and if you can't admit when you're wrong, then your relationship loses. I love the title of one marriage book, which sums it up well: *You Can Be Right, or You Can Be Married.* The book is basically about couples who could not find a way to bridge their differences and make things right again. The point is, in marriage, the relationship must take priority.

In my case, after I accept that it doesn't matter whether I am right or wrong, this is how my apology for the disrespectful tone might sound, using Heitler's six steps:

1. I'm sorry I was not respectful when I spoke to you earlier.
2. I shouldn't have talked to you that way.
3. I didn't mean to hurt your feelings.
4. I was really frustrated and should have taken a break.
5. I want you to know that I respect your opinion and want to listen to what you need.
6. Next time I'll be sure to take a break if I'm feeling angry.

Notice, I didn't say, "I'm sorry you were so offended at that." Apologizing for how our spouse reacted isn't really an apology. Dr. Frank Gunzburg, who has counseled married couples for decades, puts it this way: "Be careful when apologizing that you address your spouse's concerns and accept the blame. This will help the two of you to move beyond the mistake."

I asked Scott if he remembered any other examples of when I

have messed up and then apologized. He said, "Well, I guess that's the great thing about apologies. I don't remember." After a good apology, that's exactly the result we're going for. We don't have to remember, and we don't keep score.

The effect of a sincere apology can't be understated. As a friend of mine said, "A real apology makes the environment feel safe again." When harm has been committed and no apology offered, the space between two spouses becomes filled with distrust and tension. On the other hand, when we know our spouse has expressed remorse and committed to change, we can trust and be close again. The slate has been wiped clean. No one is perfect, but with a sincere apology, we can continually commit to be better.

Apologies can be quick, easy, and frequent in marriage if both people are always ready to make things right. I asked my brother-in-law for his thoughts on apologies, particularly because he has a lot of leadership experience, including high school student body president and college rugby team captain. He said, "That's just an important life skill—being able to own a mistake and apologize without excuse. We don't try to shift the blame and explain it away by saying 'Well, I didn't mean that.' Little things in marriage can be worked through quickly and easily if you have two sides that are willing to say sorry and take responsibility."

Here's a simple example: The other night, Scott offered to take the kids so I could go to a bookstore and write. I would be out past the kids' bedtime. I was so grateful, but as I was leaving, I said to him, "It sure would be nice if the kids aren't running around with you asleep on the couch when I get home." There's a history there, but that's beside the point. The important thing is that Scott offered to do a kind thing for me, and I left with a comment that was less than complimentary. In fact, he could easily have been offended by the suggestion. He didn't say anything.

I only realized the blunder as I was driving, and when I got to the bookstore, I sent a text saying: "Sorry about the couch comment. It's fine if the kids are hanging from the ceiling fan when I get home. I'm just really grateful you are giving me this time." Scott appreciated the gesture and was quick to forgive. Luckily, he hadn't taken offense in the first place—another perk of our regular communication of love. (I should note that the kids were snug in their beds when I got home, too.)

It doesn't take long to do, but a constant readiness to apologize can keep walls from separating you from your spouse. If you find yourself in the situation where you are the one who regularly apologizes first (or are the only one apologizing), then try having a conversation with your spouse about it. Help him or her know that you need more balance. Ultimately, if both partners are committed to apologizing whenever they have hurt their spouse, intentionally or not, then their relationship wins. That simple act will help keep your fire burning brightly.

Be fast to forgive

I recently was in a car accident that was bad enough to total our favorite family car—the one we had picked out together when our third child was born and we needed more room. What's worse, I was at fault in the accident. I had been sitting in an intersection, waiting for the traffic and ready to make a left-hand turn, when the first lane of cars stopped to let me through. I thought the coast was clear. I don't know how I missed the car in the far lane, but I just didn't see it until it was too late. We collided. I pulled off to the side of the road, shaken and scared. The first thing I thought to do was call Scott. He happened to be coming my way and was there within five minutes. When he walked over to me, he simply put his arms around me while I cried. I said over and over, "I'm so sorry, Scott. I'm so sorry." In that moment, he could have asked "What were you thinking?" or "How could you let this happen?" He didn't. He just held me and said, "It's OK." Never once did he ask me to explain myself or berate me for the time, expense, and hassle the following four weeks would bring. He forgave me on the spot and never looked back.

Scott's forgiveness was an incredible gift to me. But more than that, it was a gift to both of us. If you look up the word *forgive* in the dictionary, this is what you will find: "to stop feeling anger (toward someone who has done something wrong); to stop feeling anger about (something); to cease to feel resentment against (an offender)." Did you notice who benefits from forgiveness? It is not simply a gift for your spouse, who made the mistake. Forgiveness is also a gift for you.

One of the most amazing stories of forgiveness I know comes from the experience of a man named Chris Williams. His pregnant wife and child were killed in a car accident with a drunk driver. Rather than harboring hatred toward this young driver, Chris somehow found a way to forgive. How he could do this is beyond me; I can't imagine the grief he must have suffered. As he said in an interview with the local paper, when he realized that he had let go of the anger and forgiven the young man, "there was this immediate new perspective, a realization that I could be OK. . . . One of the great blessings of forgiveness is it allows the tragedy to stop. It doesn't need any more lives wasted." Because of his forgiving heart, Chris has been able to heal and have a loving family life again. Without that forgiveness, the bitterness could have truly ruined the rest of his life.

The same principle applies in marriage, where we are so intimately familiar with each other's flaws. Apologies are important, but apologies go nowhere without a spouse who can willingly forgive. Consider the husband who doesn't make it to his daughter's dance recital, even though he said he would. If he is genuinely sorry and says so, and he wants to do something to make it right, what good will it do for his wife to say "Well, it's not OK" and refuse to forgive him? Or consider the wife who yells at her husband and then asks to be forgiven. If he can't forgive her, then he is just as much to blame as she is for adding tension to the space between them.

Forgiveness is a choice to move forward. Here's how Fred Luskin, director of the Stanford University Forgiveness Project, explains it: "All of forgiveness work is about us, not them. And all of forgiveness work is to widen our hearts. It's not to change somebody else. It's to recognize that part of the problem is that we bring to our relationships a Grinch heart—a heart that's a couple of sizes too small—that makes us more demanding than is necessary, that makes us insensitive to the flaws of the people we have chosen to love."

Intimate relationships are so unique and important because we don't just sign up to enjoy the good things about our spouse. We sign up to accept the bad, too. If we aren't willing to do that, then "that's not intimacy," Dr. Luskin says. "Intimacy does involve taking what's pleasant, but that's no big deal. Most of us are willing to take what's pleasant from people. It's a rare person who will choose to take what's unpleasant from another person. It doesn't mean we have to be abused or mistreated, but in an intimate relationship we're going to get the full person."

Our choice in marriage is to accept everything about the person we signed up to love, or else suffer the consequences of "unforgiveness."

According to Dr. Everett L. Worthington Jr., psychology professor and director of the Campaign for Forgiveness Research, unforgiveness is "a negative emotional state where an offended person maintains feelings of resentment, hostility, anger, and hatred toward the person who offended him." Unforgiveness not only affects the health of the relationship but also the health of the person who chooses to hold on to those negative emotions. Research shows that unforgiveness has a significant effect on a person's physical, mental, and spiritual well-being.

Perhaps it's obvious that when an abuse is being committed repeatedly, that person can still choose to forgive, but healing will be more difficult. Forgiveness is not the same thing as trust, and trust takes time to earn. Every spouse also has to consider what Dr. Luskin calls "deal breakers." These are the offenses that are so bad that a person cannot continue in the relationship. By far, the majority of offenses in marriage are not deal breakers. They are the minor frustrations, irritants, and flaws that come with the person we love. We committed to take the good with the bad and to try every day not to let the bad get the best of us.

For those offenses that are not deal breakers, we have a choice. We can either forgive and let our relationship heal or we can hold on to that mistake and let it poison us. Being unwilling to forgive will only drive a wedge in the relationship, pushing two people apart. Indeed, marriage research by Susan Nolen-Hoeksema at Yale University suggests that a spouse who continually replays negative thoughts and frustrations, never willing to let the past go, contributes to a spiral of depression and isolation that may never turn around. Forgiveness can change everything.

As human beings, we are bound to mess up. Mistakes, frustration, conflicts, apologies, and forgiveness are all just part of having a close relationship. In marriage, we must be willing to move on together, apologizing when we are wrong and forgiving whenever we have the chance. "I'm sorry" and "I forgive you" go hand in hand. They shouldn't be terribly difficult to say, and they aren't admissions of being a bad or weak person. You aren't stronger or better for not apologizing or not forgiving. Indeed, it's probably almost always harder to apologize and to forgive than it is to stay silent, angry, and unwilling. Being willing to move on and put mistakes in the past means we prioritize the loving feelings in our marriage over anything else, even over being right. As Dr. Gunzburg put it, "An honest apology [and a forgiving heart] is a simple gift of love. Give it readily when appropriate."

Two-Minute Action Steps

(COMPLETE ONCE AND REPEAT OFTEN):

The next time you and your spouse have a conflict, be the first one to apologize for your part. Remember, your relationship is more important than being right.

The next time your spouse makes a mistake, be willing to forgive without reservation and without holding a grudge.

Chapter 11

How Do You Love Me?
A Word on Differences

Share our similarities; celebrate our differences.

—M. Scott Peck, AMERICAN AUTHOR AND PSYCHIATRIST

No one sees the world the same way. Everything that makes us who we are affects our ability to love and feel loved. If we go about loving our spouse in the way we want to be loved, we may be missing the mark. Take time to explore each other's unique needs, which stem from childhood experiences, gender differences, love languages, personalities, and passions. Understanding individual needs will help you most effectively love and appreciate your spouse.

Consider Childhood Experiences

Our history affects who we are and how we see the world. It impacts how we love and feel loved, what we see as normal, and why we sometimes feel pain. Keeping our unique childhood experiences in mind can help us better understand why we do the things we do.

Occasionally, our past can have an adverse effect on our interactions in marriage. According to Dr. Jamie Turndorf, these childhood scars can cause trouble:

- Lack of attention from parents, which can result in excessive clinginess or fear of intimacy
- Overly controlling parents, which can result in overly controlling or uncooperative behavior in adulthood
- Too much responsibility without time to play as a child, which can lead to irresponsible behavior or overly responsible behavior in adulthood
- Lack of limits or responsibility in childhood, which can lead to immature behavior
- Experiences with verbal or physical abuse in childhood, which can lead to abusive behavior or experiences in adulthood
- Feeling like parents liked a sibling better, which can lead to excessive side taking or frustration over differences of opinion[171]

Do you feel like your spouse is too controlling? Too clingy? Too immature? Look back at the past and see if you can discover an explanation. Being aware of childhood experiences can help spouses be more tolerant and understanding of behavior that might otherwise be confusing and even frustrating. That understanding can also help you work toward healing.

A friend explained to me how understanding his wife's childhood experiences helped him better understand her as a person. "We were staying with her family once, and when we were heading to bed, she just said 'Goodnight' to her mom from across the room.

I asked, 'Why didn't you go hug her?' To me, it felt unfinished and even cold, but she didn't think it was a big deal. She just didn't grow up that way." He went on to explain, "When you understand your spouse's growing-up years, it's easier to be tolerant and appreciate the differences. Knowledge is power."

Take opportunities to talk openly about childhood experiences (without placing blame or being critical). Discuss your own childhood experiences with your spouse, and talk about behaviors that might remind you of negative childhood experiences. Explore each other's unmet needs from childhood, and take time to consider how each spouse can be a part of healing. Use the knowledge of your spouse's background to gain patience and understanding during times of conflict and to show love in the ways your spouse needs it most.

Consider Differences between Men and Women

Some therapists have suggested that men and women are so different it's like we come from different planets. Have you ever looked at your spouse and thought *What in the world is she doing?* or *Why on earth doesn't he get it?* Let's face it: men and women sometimes just do things differently. This becomes clear even in childhood. Scott and I laugh sometimes watching the differences between how our sons and daughters interact with the world. When my oldest son was young, I would usually just set an outfit out on the floor for him after he took a bath. For our girls, sometimes three outfit choices on the bed just aren't enough. Then, after finally selecting the choice ensemble, they change five minutes later. Our two boys love blocks and cars, while the girls make families out of everything from dolls to ducks to spoons. I used to think that was all just stereotype, but that has definitely been our family's experience.

In marriage, it's important to understand some of the differences between men and women so we can best meet each other's needs. Some of those differences are biological. Some are a result of socialization. Dr. Willard Harley is a nationally acclaimed clinical psychologist who has studied the needs of married couples for more than thirty years, which he writes about in his international best-seller *His Needs, Her Needs: Building an Affair-Proof Marriage.* In his research, Dr. Harley has found that men and women have significantly different needs when it comes to feeling loved. For example, surveys show that for men as a group, two of the most reported needs are physical intimacy and recreational companionship. Men also report a desire to feel appreciation from their wives in order to feel fulfilled in their relationship. Feeling unappreciated can have drastic consequences, according to marriage therapist Dr. Jamie Turndorf, who says, "If you ask a man why he had an affair, 99 percent of the time it was not because he wasn't getting enough sex; it was because he wasn't receiving enough appreciation from his wife." That's not meant to put the blame on the wives' shoulders, but it is an interesting correlation. This demonstrates how desperate the need is to feel valued and appreciated.

Men are also particularly sensitive to feelings of shame, according to Dr. Patricia Love and Dr. Steven Stosney. That sensitivity can make men want to pull away when their spouse is suggesting, intentionally or not, that he is doing anything wrong. Often, the more she tries to discuss problem areas in the relationship, the more he withdraws in what John Gottman has dubbed the "nag-withdrawal syndrome." In a nutshell, research suggests that, more than anything, a husband wants to know that his wife thinks highly of him and wants to be connected to him.

Women as a group, on the other hand, are more likely to report feeling loved through affection and intimate conversation, according to Dr. Harley. They are also more biologically vulnerable than their husbands to a fear of being disconnected. Perhaps ironically, that fear makes them want to reach out to talk to their partner about improving their relationship, which can be uncomfortable for their spouse, who may interpret her unhappiness as a critique of his ability to care for her. Wives simply want to feel cared for and emotionally close to their husbands.

Understanding these different needs and vulnerabilities can help men and women focus more on effectively loving their partner. By satisfying the needs of their partner, both men and women are more likely to see their own needs met in return. As women come to understand and fulfill their husband's need for appreciation, respect, physical intimacy, and companionship, they will be more likely to have a partner who wants and is able to be emotionally intimate and connected. The reverse is also true. The more a husband is willing to be affectionate and emotionally connected with his wife, the more she can and will respond to his needs.

This research of course does not mean that every individual must fit the mold. Just because you are a man does not necessarily mean you want intimacy and recreation first and foremost, or just because you are a woman does not necessarily mean you are inclined toward wanting late-night chats. You might be the opposite. These findings are just a starting point for a conversation about your relationship. Maybe when you think it over, you will see differences relating to gender you hadn't thought of before. Ask yourself, and your spouse, how each of you most feels loved. What matters most is having the desire to meet your partner's needs, even if those needs are different from your own.

Consider Love Languages

Have you ever considered how your spouse feels loved? Does she light up when you do the dishes after dinner? Does he love it when you surprise him with a kiss? Is more time together her biggest request? Have you ever wondered if your spouse feels love differently than you do? According to marriage counselor Dr. Gary Chapman, just as people speak different languages around the world, people also feel love in different ways. If we aren't speaking the right love language, all our efforts may fall flat. Essential in making your spouse feel loved is knowing what love language to use. These are the five love languages according to Dr. Chapman:

- Words of affirmation (words of praise, respect, and gratitude)
- Acts of service (doing thoughtful things to help and serve your spouse)
- Receiving gifts (bringing home a surprise for your spouse)
- Quality time (spending time talking and doing activities together)
- Physical touch (physical closeness, including massage, hugging, kissing, holding hands, and physical intimacy)

One of my favorite speakers, John Bytheway, described when he finally realized that he and his wife did not speak the same love language. He had been taking her car to get washed, regularly, because he really likes having a clean car. He knew he would love it if his wife did that for him. It was some time later that it finally came out: although she appreciated his efforts, what she really wanted was flowers.

I, like most of us, respond well to all of the love languages. I love it when Scott brings me flowers, our time together, hearing sweet words, and physical touch. Those things are all wonderful opportunities for us to deepen our connection and strengthen our affection. But the way I feel loved most is when Scott is doing the dishes, cooking a meal, or helping our kids. Acts of service melt me like nothing else. Consider the difference between Scott knowing what that means to me and him not having a clue. Knowing how much I love that apron on him when he's scrubbing away at the sink allows him to enjoy bringing me that pleasure (well, at least as much as anyone can reasonably enjoy doing the dishes).

We can all do ourselves a favor by sitting down with our spouse and figuring some things out. Talk. Listen. Explore. How do you each feel loved? Do you most feel it when your spouse thanks you or tells you how much he loves you? Or do you love it when your spouse does something nice for you? What about when he brings home a little surprise just for you? Is it spending time together that makes you feel loved? Is it when she rubs your back? Figure out what each of you most appreciates, and be sure to speak that language regularly.

Consider Passions and Personalities

Two more areas where spouses can be as different as night and day are in their passions and personalities. Take a moment to think about how you are different from your spouse in your likes, dislikes, interests, tendencies, strengths, and weaknesses. Recognizing how you are different can help you better understand and appreciate each other. For example, Scott is an obvious extrovert: he enjoys parties and meeting new people. I'd rather be home with a good book. He wakes up early, and I love sleeping in. His dream vacation is taking our family to see a string of national parks in an RV. Mine can be summed up in two words: beach house. We can choose to let our differences irritate us and drive us apart, or we can enjoy the diversity in our marriage, allowing ourselves to see new perspectives and try new things.

One way to learn more about the differences in your personalities and interests is to have a conversation about them. If you don't already know, just ask each other: Ocean or mountains? Party animal or bookworm? Take a risk or play it safe? Modern or traditional? Night owl or early bird? Workaholic or free spirit? Logical or emotional? Brainstorm everything you can think of. You might be surprised to learn some things you never knew.

Take it a step further and try an online personality test. Many are available, including the color test, the Myers-Briggs, the Big Five, and an ongoing study called the Synthetic Aperture Personality Assessment (or SAPA). My favorite test for use in relationships is the Jung Typology Test, which is based on four dichotomies of personality: introversion/extroversion, intuition/sensing, thinking/feeling, and judging/perception. The test results in a four-letter code that describes the participant as one of 16 personality types. You can use this test to discover more about yourself and the areas where you and your spouse differ (there's even a marriage analysis option for a small fee that can zone in on potential conflict areas based on your personality reports). A free test is available at www.humanmetrics.com.

Differences are a part of life. They add variety and keep things interesting. No one wants a box of crayons with just one color, right? Sure, life might be easier if we were just the same as our spouse. But "easy" isn't what makes marriage so rewarding. Celebrate your differences, and seek understanding when those differences cause conflicts. Remember, those are often the times that give us the chance to grow as we try to experience the world in someone else's shoes.

Two-Minute Action Steps

(COMPLETE ONCE AND REPEAT OFTEN):

Ask yourself and your partner: "How did you feel most loved when you were growing up?" and "Was there any type of affection or interaction with your parents you didn't receive when you were growing up that you wish you had (e.g., more willingness to listen or spend time together, more rules or structure, more free time to play and be a child)?"

To better understand each other's needs, ask yourself and your partner: "In which of these ten ways do you feel most loved (from Dr. William Harley's *His Needs, Her Needs*)?" Be sure to love your spouse with their choices in mind:

- Affection (kindness and emotional closeness)
- Intimate conversation
- Physical intimacy
- Recreational companionship
- Honesty and openness
- An attractive spouse
- Domestic support (having help around the house)
- Financial commitment (being provided for financially)
- Admiration
- Family commitment

Ask yourself and your partner: "Which of these best describes your love language (from Dr. Gary Chapman's *The Five Love Languages*)?" Be sure to speak that language often:

- Words of affirmation (expressions of love and gratitude)
- Time together
- Acts of service
- Gifts
- Physical touch

Discuss with your spouse how your interests and personalities differ. Consider taking a personality test. Ask yourselves, how could recognizing your differences help you better understand and appreciate one another?

Commit to loving your spouse in many different ways every day. Focus especially on the ways he or she feels most loved and be tolerant of areas where you differ.

Chapter 12

Carry On: Love Is a Verb

The "secret" to loving is loving: the more we give
of that vast and powerful force called Love, the
more it returns to illuminate our days with hope,
simple bliss, and heart-happy wonder.

—Margie Lapanja, American author

Finding the one you want to love for the rest of your life is a gift. As with many other precious things in life, the reward of a lasting and joyful partnership doesn't come without effort. Staying in love demands a price of unfailing commitment and deliberate action. With a million forces pulling our attention in other directions, we have to fight for the relationship that matters most. If we can commit to loving our spouse in little ways, through thick and thin, every day of our marriage, then we can have everything we hoped for when we said "I do."

In marriage, love is more than a feeling. Love is a verb. One isolated act of love here or there probably won't do much. Over time, many small acts every day will keep you connected. The efforts you make to show love, respect, and gratitude to your spouse every day over weeks and months and years can make the

179

difference between two disconnected people living under one roof and an affectionate union of two best friends, lovers, and soul mates. The more we can make these positive, loving connections with our spouse, the better. Indeed, Dr. John Gottman's "magic ratio" for a happy marriage is 5 to 1. Couples, he says, should have five times as many positive interactions as negative ones. The book in your hands is chock-full of simple ways to create those loving interactions.

Finding ways to connect is possible even when everyone is busy and time is scarce. Consider the marriage in which the husband works long hours but he and his wife still find simple ways to show their love. As Dr. Gottman writes, "When [Olivia] has a doctor's appointment, [Nathaniel] remembers to call to see how it went. When he has a meeting with an important client, she'll check in to see how it fared. When they have chicken for dinner, she gives him both drumsticks because she knows he likes them best. When he makes blueberry pancakes for the kids Saturday morning, he leaves the blueberries out of hers because he knows she doesn't like them." Dr. Gottman goes on to summarize the importance of these little gestures: "If all of this sounds humdrum and unromantic, it's anything but. Through small but important ways, Olivia and Nathaniel are maintaining the friendship that is the foundation of their love. As a result, they have a marriage that is far more passionate than do couples who punctuate their lives together with romantic vacations and lavish anniversary gifts but have fallen out of touch in their daily lives." It is the everyday, *small and simple things* that keep us in love.

Think about everything your marriage has to offer you: someone to laugh with; someone to share secrets with; someone to share sorrows with; someone to hope for the future with; perhaps someone to experience all the joys of having children and grandchildren with; someone to grow old with, travel with, and just *do life* with; and someone to love who loves you in return. It may not come easy, but as Dr. John Jacobs explains, it is more than worth it: "My work over twenty years as a marriage therapist has taught me that a good marriage, a marriage that supports and gratifies both spouses, is more difficult to achieve and sustain than most people are willing to believe. Nonetheless, if you're willing to work conscientiously and continually to have a loving relationship, you can attain it, and you'll find it among the most fulfilling achievements of your adult life." Invest in these simple secrets. You will never regret the moments you dedicated to your marriage.

The other night, Scott had gone to bed early after being up late working the night before. I was on the computer when I looked up to see he had left his protein shake bottles dirty on the counter. My first thought was, "Is it so hard to put those in the dishwasher?" My next thought was, "Well, here's an opportunity." I shut down the computer, rinsed out the bottles, and put them in the dishwasher so they would be ready for him in the morning. I knew he'd appreciate that. I walked up the stairs to the bathroom. When I went to grab my toothbrush, I noticed it there on the sink, toothpaste already spread. I smiled, knowing it was Scott who put it there. I brushed my teeth, turned out the lights, and crawled in bed next to him. Sleepily, he flopped an arm over me and pulled me close. I closed my eyes and thought to myself, "Maybe that's what it all comes down to. Staying in love isn't rocket science. It is just *this*. If you want to stay in love . . . then keep loving."

Sources

Preface

Bruess, Carol J., and Anna D. H. Kudak. *What Happy Couples Do: Belly Button Fuzz & Bare-Chested Hugs*. Minneapolis, MN: Fairview Press, 2008.

Gottman, John, and Julie Gottman. *10 Lessons to Transform Your Marriage: America's Love Lab Experts Share Their Strategies for Strengthening Your Relationship*. New York: Crown Publishers, 2006.

Jacobs, John W. *All You Need Is Love & Other Lies about Marriage: How to Save Your Marriage Before It's Too Late*. New York: HarperCollins, 2004.

Parker-Pope, Tara. *For Better: The Science of a Good Marriage*. New York: Penguin Group, 2010.

Chapter 1

Brody, Jane. "That Loving Feeling Takes a Lot of Work." *New York Times Blogs*. http://well.blogs.nytimes.com/2013/01/14/that-loving-feeling-takes-a-lot-of-work.

Coontz, Stephanie. *Marriage, a History: How Love Conquered Marriage*. New York: Penguin Books, 2006.

Fetsch, R. J., and B. Jacobson. "Dealing with Couples' Anger." April 2007. Last modified April 19, 2013. http://www.ext.colostate.edu/pubs/consumer/10238.html.

Gottman, John, and Robert Levenson. "The Timing of Divorce: Predicting When a Couple Will Divorce Over a 14-Year Period." *Journal of Marriage and the Family* 62 (2000): 737-745. http://ist-socrates.berkeley.edu/~ucbpl/docs/61-Timing%20of%20Divorce00.pdf.

Gottman, John, and Julie Gottman. *10 Lessons to Transform Your Marriage: America's Love Lab Experts Share Their Strategies for Strengthening Your Relationship*. New York: Crown Publishers, 2006.

Haag, Pamela. *Marriage Confidential: The Post-Romantic Age of Workhorse Wives, Royal Children, Undersexed Spouses, and Rebel Couples Who Are Rewriting the Rules.* New York: Harper, 2011.

Hendrix, Harville, and Helen LaKelly Hunt. *Making Marriage Simple: Ten Relationship-Saving Truths.* New York: Crown Publishers, 2013.

Jacobs, John W. *All You Need Is Love & Other Lies about Marriage: How to Save Your Marriage Before It's Too Late.* New York: HarperCollins, 2004.

Lyubomirsky, Sonja. *The Myths of Happiness: What Should Make You Happy but Doesn't; What Shouldn't Make You Happy but Does.* New York: Penguin Group, 2013.

Parker-Pope, Tara. *For Better: The Science of a Good Marriage.* New York: Penguin Group, 2010.

Streisand, Barbra, and Bryan Adams. "I Finally Found Someone." *The Mirror Has Two Faces.* 1996.

Chapter 2

Bruess, Carol J., and Anna D. H. Kudak. *What Happy Couples Do: Belly Button Fuzz & Bare-Chested Hugs.* Minneapolis, MN: Fairview Press, 2008.

Hallowell, Edward M., and Sue George Hallowell. *Married to Distraction: Restoring Intimacy and Strengthening Your Marriage in an Age of Interruption.* New York: Ballantine Books, 2010.

How to Lose a Guy in Ten Days. Dir. Donald Petrie. 2003. Paramount Pictures.

Parker-Pope, Tara. *For Better: The Science of a Good Marriage.* New York: Penguin Group, 2010.

Chapter 3

Bruess, Carol J., and Anna D. H. Kudak. *What Happy Couples Do: Belly Button Fuzz & Bare-Chested Hugs.* Minneapolis, MN: Fairview Press, 2008.

Emmons, Robert. *Thanks!: How the New Science of Gratitude Can Make You Happier.* Boston: Houghton Mifflin Harcourt, 2007.

Gottman, John, and Julie Gottman. *10 Lessons to Transform Your Marriage: America's Love Lab Experts Share Their Strategies for Strengthening Your Relationship.* New York: Crown Publishers, 2006.

Gottman, John and Nan Silver. *The Seven Principles for Making Marriage Work.* New York: Crown Publishing, 2000.

Gunzberg, Frank. "Attitude Is Everything: Your Attitude Determines Your Feelings and Actions." 1999. www.marriage-counselor.com/attitude-is-everything.

Happy. Dir. Roko Belic. 2011. Wadi Rum Films.

Rosenthal, Robert, and Jacobson, L. 1968. *Pygmalion in the Classroom.* New York: Holt, Rinehart & Winston.

Seligman, Martin. *Authentic Happiness: Using the New Positive Psychology to Realize Your Potential for Lasting Fulfillment.* New York: Atria Books, 2004.

Chapter 4

Bruess, Carol J., and Anna D. H. Kudak. *What Happy Couples Do: Belly Button Fuzz & Bare-Chested Hugs.* Minneapolis, MN: Fairview Press, 2008.

Burns, Jim. *Creating an Intimate Marriage.* Minneapolis, MN: Bethany House Publishers, 2006.

Ganesan, P. C. *Winners Make it Happen.* Tamil Nadu, India: Sura Books, 2010.

Gottman, John, and Nan Silver. *The Seven Principles for Making Marriage Work.* New York: Crown Publishing, 2000.

Heitler, Susan. *The Power of Two: Secrets to a Strong and Loving Marriage.* Oakland: New Harbinger Publications, 1997.

Hendrix, Harville, and Helen LaKelly Hunt. *Making Marriage Simple.* New York: Crown Publishers, 2013.

Kowal, Elizabeth, "Oxytocin, the Love Hormone, Has Health Benefits for Both Genders." *Health & Fitness*, Oct. 24, 2009.

The Mirror Has Two Faces. Dir. Barbara Streisand. 1996. TriStar Pictures.

Parker-Pope, Tara. *For Better: The Science of a Good Marriage*. New York: Penguin Group, 2010.

Chapter 5

Adams, Amy. "How Does She Know?" *Enchanted*. 2007.

Adams, Bryan. "(Everything I Do) I Do It for You." 1991.

Baumgardner, Julie. "The Power of Prayer in Marriage." *First Things First*.

Brimhall, Andrew. "Benefits of Couple Prayer." *Forever Families*. https://foreverfamilies.byu.edu/Pages/marriage/SpiritualStrength/Benefits-of-Couple-Prayer.aspx.

Bruess, Carol J., and Anna D. H. Kudak. *What Happy Couples Do: Belly Button Fuzz & Bare-Chested Hugs*. Minneapolis, MN: Fairview Press, 2008.

Chapman, Gary. *The Five Love Languages*. Chicago, IL: Northfield Publishing, 2010.

Dr. Seuss. *The Sneeches and Other Stories*. "The Zax." New York: Random House, 1961.

Gottman, John, and Nan Silver. *The Seven Principles for Making Marriage Work*. New York: Crown Publishing, 2000.

Gottman, John, and Robert Levenson. "The Timing of Divorce: Predicting When a Couple Will Divorce Over a 14-Year Period." *Journal of Marriage and the Family* 62 (2000): 737-745. http://conium.org/~ucbpl/docs/61-Timing%20of%20Divorce00.pdf.

Gottman, John and Julie Gottman. *10 Lessons to Transform Your Marriage: America's Love Lab Experts Share Their Strategies for Strengthening Your Relationship*. New York: Crown Publishers, 2006.

Jayson, Sharon. "Married Couples Who Play Together Stay Together." *USA Today*, July 17, 2008. http://usatoday30.usatoday.com/news/nation/2008-07-15-fun-in-marriage_N.htm.

Klein, Wendy, Carolina Izquierdo, and Thomas Bradbury. "The Difference Between a Happy Marriage and a Miserable One: Chores." *The Atlantic,* March 1, 2013. http://www.theatlantic.com/sexes/archive/2013/03/the-difference-between-a-happy-marriage-and-miserable-one-chores/273615/.

Lambert, Nathanial. "Praying Together and Staying Together: Couple Prayer and Trust" http://www.fincham.info/papers/2012-prs-pray-together.pdf

Lyubomirsky, Sonja. *The Myths of Happiness: What Should Make You Happy but Doesn't; What Shouldn't Make You Happy but Does.* New York: Penguin Group, 2013.

Lyubomirsky, Sonja. *The How of Happiness: A New Approach to Getting the Life You Want.* New York: Penguin Group, 2008.

Meltzer, Andrea L.; James K. McNulty, Grace L. Jackson, and Benjamin R. Karney. "Sex Differences in the Implications of Partner Physical Attractiveness for the Trajectory of Marital Satisfaction." *Journal of Personality and Social Psychology.* Vol 106(3). March 2014. 418-428.

Parrott, Les, and Leslie Parrott. *Saving Your Marriage Before It Starts: Seven Questions to Ask before—and—after You Marry.* Grand Rapids, MI: Zondervan, 2006.

Smith, Emily Esfahani. "Masters of Love." *The Atlantic,* June 12, 2014. http://www.theatlantic.com/health/archive/2014/06/happily-ever-after/372573.

Chapter 6

"Being a Social Media Junkie May Not Be Good for Your Marriage: Study." *Daily News,* April 12, 2013. http://www.nydailynews.com/life-style/social-media-harm-marriage-article-1.1315245.

Chumley, Cheryl K. "Facebook Cited in a Third of All Divorce Cases: 'It's like having a massive public noticeboard.'" *The Washington Times,* January 21, 2015. http://www.washingtontimes.com/news/2015/jan/21/facebook-cited-in-a-third-of-all-divorce-cases-its/.

Collier, Hatty. "Women Prefer Their Smartphone to Their Partner, Study Finds." *Evening Standard*, October 13, 2016. http://www.standard. co.uk/news/techandgadgets/women-spend-more-time-on-their-smartphone-than-with-their-partner-study-finds-a3367856.html.

Hadfield, Joe. "Online Role-Playing Games Hurt Marital Satisfaction, Says BYU Study." *BYU News*. February 13, 2012. https://news.byu.edu/ news/online-role-playing-games-hurt-marital-satisfaction-says-byu-study.

Kleponis, Peter. "The Effects of Pornography on Wives and Marriages." *Covenant Eyes*, July 6, 2010. http://www.covenanteyes. com/2010/07/06/the-effects-of-pornography-on-wives-and-marriages.

Manning J., Senate Testimony 2004, referencing: Dedmon, J., "Is the Internet bad for your marriage? Online affairs, pornographic sites playing greater role in divorces," 2002, press release from the American Academy of Matrimonial Lawyers.

Pew Internet Project. "Social Networking Fact Sheet." *Pew Research Center*, December 27, 2013. http://www.pewinternet.org/fact-sheets/social-networking-fact-sheet/.

Skinner, Kevin B. "Is Porn Really Destroying 500,000 Marriages Annually?" *Psychology Today*, December 12, 2011. https://www.psychologytoday. com/blog/inside-porn-addiction/201112/is-porn-really-destroying-500000-marriages-annually.

Wong, Brittany. "7 Ways Facebook Can Ruin Your Relationship." *The Huffington Post*, December 16, 2015. http://www.huffingtonpost. com/entry/7-ways-facebook-can-ruin-your-relationship_us_56706867e4b0e292150f80b6.

Chapter 7

Allred, Hugh G. *How to Strengthen Your Marriage and Family*. Provo, UT: Brigham Young University Press, 1976.

Burns, Jim. *Creating an Intimate Marriage*. Minneapolis, MN: Bethany House Publishers, 2006.

Dineen, Cari Wira. "The Hidden Health Benefits of Sex." *Women's Health Magazine*, March. 15, 2013. http://www.womenshealthmag.com/health/health-benefits-of-sex.

Gottman, John, and Nan Silver. *The Seven Principles for Making Marriage Work*. New York: Crown Publishing, 2000.

Harley, Jr., Willard F. *His Needs, Her Needs: Building an Affair-Proof Marriage*. Grand Rapids, MI: Baker Publishing Group, 2001.

Hendrix, Harville, and Helen LaKelly Hunt. *Making Marriage Simple*. New York: Crown Publishers, 2013.

Lyubomirsky, Sonja. *The Myths of Happiness: What Should Make You Happy but Doesn't; What Shouldn't Make You Happy but Does*. New York: Penguin Group, 2013.

Schnarch, David. *Intimacy and Desire: Awaken the Passion in Your Relationship*. New York: Beaufort Books, 2009.

Chapter 8

Anwar, Yasmin. "Wives Matter More When It Comes to Calming Down Marital Conflicts." *UC Berkeley News*, November 4, 2013. http://news.berkeley.edu/2013/11/04/marriage-peacekeepers/.

Chapman, Gary. *The Five Love Languages*. Chicago, IL: Northfield Publishing, 2010.

Covey, Stephen R. *The 7 Habits of Highly Effective People: Powerful Lessons in Personal Change*. New York: Fireside, 1989.

Gottman, John, and Julie Gottman. *10 Lessons to Transform Your Marriage: America's Love Lab Experts Share Their Strategies for Strengthening Your Relationship*. New York: Crown Publishers, 2006.

Gottman, John, and Nan Silver. *The Seven Principles for Making Marriage Work*. New York: Crown Publishing, 2000.

Gray, John. *Men Are from Mars, Women Are from Venus: The Classic Guide to Understanding the Opposite Sex*. New York: HarperCollins, 1992.

Love, Patricia, and Steven Stosny. *How to Improve Your Marriage Without Talking About It*. New York: Broadway Books, 2007.

Parker-Pope, Tara. *For Better: The Science of a Good Marriage*. New York: Penguin Group, 2010.

Patterson, Kerry, Joseph Grenny, Ron McMillan, and Al Switzler. *Crucial Conversations: Tools for Talking When Stakes Are High*. New York: McGraw-Hill, 2002.

Real, Terrence. *The New Rules of Marriage: A Breakthrough Program For 21st-Century Relationships*. New York: Ballantine Books, 2007.

Smith, Emily Esfahani. "Masters of Love." *The Atlantic*, June 12, 2014. http://www.theatlantic.com/health/archive/2014/06/happily-ever-after/372573.

Turndorf, Jamie. *Till Death Do Us Part (Unless I Kill You First): A Step-by-Step Guide for Resolving Relationship Conflict*. Charleston, SC: BookSurge Publishing, 2009.

Chapter 9

Father of the Bride. Dir. Charles Shyer. 1991. Sandollar Productions.

Gottman, John. *Why Marriages Succeed or Fail . . . And How You Can Make Yours Last*. New York, NY: Simon & Schuster, 1995.

Erikson, Jenny. "10 Things to Say If You Want to Destroy Your Marriage." *The Stir Blog*, November 18, 2013. http://thestir.cafemom.com/love_sex/164334/10_things_to_say_if.

Gottman, John, and Nan Silver. *The Seven Principles for Making Marriage Work*. New York: Crown Publishing, 2000.

Harley, Jr., Willard F. *His Needs, Her Needs: Building an Affair-Proof Marriage*. Grand Rapids, MI: Baker Publishing Group, 2001.

Turndorf, Jamie. *Till Death Do Us Part (Unless I Kill You First): A Step-by-Step Guide for Resolving Relationship Conflict*. Charleston, SC: BookSurge Publishing, 2009.

Chapter 10

Gottman, John, and Julie Gottman. *10 Lessons to Transform Your Marriage: America's Love Lab Experts Share Their Strategies for Strengthening Your Relationship*. New York: Crown Publishers, 2006.

Gunzberg, Frank. "Apologize Already." 1999. www.marriage-counselor-doctor.com/apologize-already.

Heitler, Susan. *The Power of Two: Secrets to a Strong and Loving Marriage.* Oakland: New Harbinger Publications, 1997.

Henrie, Jessica. "Father relies on faith to forgive intoxicated teen driver." *Deseret News*, Aug. 1, 2012. http://www.deseretnews.com/article/865559847/Let-It-Go-Chris-Williams-shares-his-story-of-tragedy-and-forgiveness.html?pg=all.

Luskin, Fred. "Fred Luskin on Overcoming the Pain of Intimacy." *Greater Good: The Science of a Meaningful Life*, February, 11, 2012. http://greatergood.berkeley.edu/article/item/fred_luskin_on_overcoming_the_pain_of_intimacy.

Shapiro, Dana Adam. *You Can Be Right or You Can Be Married: Looking for Love in the Age of Divorce*. New York: Simon & Schuster, 2012.

Worthington, Everett L. "The New Science of Forgiveness." *Greater Good: The Science of a Meaningful Life*, September 1, 2004. http://greatergood.berkeley.edu/article/item/the_new_science_of_forgiveness.

Chapter 11

Bytheway, John. *5 Things You Can Do Today to Bless Your Marriage*. Salt Lake City, UT: Deseret Book, 2010.

Chapman, Gary. *The Five Love Languages*. Chicago, IL: Northfield Publishing, 2010.

Harley Jr., Willard F. *His Needs, Her Needs: Building an Affair-Proof Marriage*. Grand Rapids, MI: Baker Publishing Group, 2001.

Love, Patricia, and Steven Stosny. *How to Improve Your Marriage Without Talking About It*. New York: Broadway Books, 2007.

Turndorf, Jamie. *Till Death Do Us Part (Unless I Kill You First): A Step-by-Step Guide for Resolving Relationship Conflict*. Charleston, SC: BookSurge Publishing, 2009.

Chapter 12

Gottman, John. *Why Marriages Succeed or Fail . . . And How You Can Make Yours Last.* New York, NY: Simon & Schuster, 1995.

Gottman, John, and Nan Silver. *The Seven Principles for Making Marriage Work.* New York: Crown Publishing, 2000.

Jacobs, John W. *All You Need Is Love & Other Lies about Marriage: How to Save Your Marriage Before It's Too Late.* New York: HarperCollins, 2004.

Acknowledgments

Thanks to my dear family and friends who helped shape this book with their staying-in-love stories. Thanks to Familius—and my editor, Katie Arnold—for their dedication to bringing happiness to families and for making this dream a reality. Thanks to Susie Taylor, Bob Taylor, Kerry Hardy, Lindsay Poelman, and Kent Griffiths for reading the manuscript and offering such helpful feedback. Most of all, thanks to Scott for encouraging this project, for giving me time to write, for brainstorming ideas with me, for reviewing each chapter, and for teaching me so much about love. You are my hero, my best friend, and my inspiration. This was only possible because of you.

About the Author

Heidi Poelman received her degrees in communication from Brigham Young University (BA) and Wake Forest University (MA). In graduate school, she focused specifically on interpersonal communication and conflict management. She loves researching and writing about subjects that help strengthen families. In addition to *The Two-Minute Secret for Staying In Love*, Heidi is the author of *A Mother's Greatest Gift: Relying on the Spirit as You Raise Your Children* and the children's book *A is for Abinadi: An Alphabet Book of Scripture Heroes*. She lives in Utah with her husband and four children. Learn more at www.heidipoelman.com.

About Familius

Welcome to a place where mothers are celebrated, not compared. Where heart is at the center of our families, and family at the center of our homes. Where boo boos are still kissed, cake beaters are still licked, and mistakes are still okay. Welcome to a place where books—and family—are beautiful. Familius: a book publisher dedicated to helping families be happy.

Visit Our Website: www.familius.com

Our website is a different kind of place. Get inspired, read articles, discover books, watch videos, connect with our family experts, download books and apps and audiobooks, and along the way, discover how values and happy family life go together.

Join Our Family

There are lots of ways to connect with us! Subscribe to our newsletters at www.familius.com to receive uplifting daily inspiration, essays from our Pater Familius, a free ebook every month, and the first word on special discounts and Familius news.

Get Bulk Discounts

If you feel a few friends and family might benefit from what you've read, let us know and we'll be happy to provide you with quantity discounts. Simply e-mail us at orders@familius.com.

Website: www.familius.com
Facebook: www.facebook.com/paterfamilius
Twitter: @familiustalk, @paterfamilius1
Pinterest: www.pinterest.com/familius

CPSIA information can be obtained
at www.ICGtesting.com
Printed in the USA
FSOW02n2115241117
41451FS

9 781945 547058